A HISTORY TODAY BOOK

The Impact of The English Civil War

D0107722

A HISTORY TODAY BOOK

The Impact of the English Civil War

EDITED BY JOHN MORRILL

COLLINS & BROWN

First published in Great Britain in 1991
by Collins & Brown Limited
Mercury House
195 Knightsbridge
London SW7 1RE

A CIP catalogue record for this book
is available from the British Library

ISBN 1 85585 042 7

Typeset by Falcon Graphic Art Ltd, Wallington, Surrey
Printed and bound in Great Britain by The Bath Press, Avon

Contents

Preface

This book has been conceived as a unity. The authors have liaised with one another in an attempt to ensure that as much ground as possible is covered without significant overlap, and I wish to express my gratitude to all of them for delivering their texts on time, keeping within the draconian word limits, and taking editorial direction in such good spirit. (I confess that I felt at times like one of those slightly bumptious officials at stately homes who are employed to make everyone park their cars neatly in order to squeeze visitors into a car park of limited size and unlikely shape!)

The book is designed to offer the fruits of the best recent research in an economical and effective way. Each information box is designed either to offer a definition of a complex historical term without clogging the text with lengthy definitions, or to offer, through quotations, some vivid examples of points made in the text. The pictures are not just adornments, but are designed to offer an economical way of highlighting or nuancing the text. They were chosen by the authors as they composed their chapters, to be intrinsic to what they are trying to communicate. Several of the authors have said how much they *enjoyed* writing these essays. There was a challenge about trying to condense whole areas of study into a very tight form of writing. I hope some of their pleasure of discovery about this most exhilarating period of English history will communicate itself from the authors to the readers.

October 1990   JOHN MORRILL

Introduction

JOHN MORRILL

Historians have had no difficulty in agreeing on what to call the events in France in and after 1789, or in Russia in and after 1917; or, in the earlier modern period, to label the political and religious schisms of the sixteenth century the Reformation, or the social, political and religious conflicts in France in the later sixteenth century the Wars of Religion.

Yet there never has been any agreement amongst historians about what to call the crisis in England in the 1640s. Contemporaries in England saw it as 'the Troubles' or as 'the Great Civil War' or as the 'Great Rebellion'; while contemporaries in Scotland saw it as the 'Wars of the Covenant' and contemporaries in Ireland as the 'War of Three Kingdoms'. Nineteenth-century historians called it the 'Puritan Revolution', and twentieth-century historians, seeing it as the precursor of the other great world revolutions, have seen it as the 'English Revolution'. New titles are still being sought by scholars hard pressed for a good book title. The most recent attempts are 'England's Wars of Religion' and 'the Last Baronial Revolt'.

This terminological confusion is itself an indication of the sheer complexity of the crisis that overwhelmed the kingdoms of Charles I in the years after 1640; and the fact is that each of the above titles *does* describe a crucial dimension of an immensely complex process.

To some extent the titles describe different events, or at any rate locate the centre of gravity at different times. Some historians see things as flowing remorselessly from Charles's loss of the initiative in 1640, when he was compelled by Scottish military demands to summon a Parliament dominated by men determined to bring an end to his mild tyranny of the 1630s, his undermining of the Protestant identity of the English Church and his exposing of his people to threats from the international popish conspiracy. Others have concentrated on the crisis of 1642, when the nation divided and armies formed. Such historians assert that what has to be explained is how, given the determination of the majority to avoid getting drawn into a war, the nation was sucked into conflict by two militant minorities. The first was made up of those persuaded that the concessions wrung from Charles were sufficient to safeguard liberties. Such men were also convinced that there was a real threat of social anarchy and religious chaos if order was not quickly restored. The other party was made up of those convinced of the insincerity of Charles's acceptance of the remedial legislation of 1641 and it was committed either to surrounding the King with honest and reliable counsellors (a King lacking personal judgement must not be allowed to judge who was to inform his judgement), or to reforming the Reformation – that is, to completing the process by which the superstition and idolatry of the

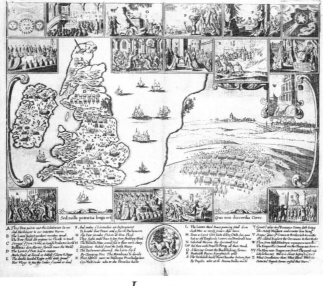

Images of war.

Old Religions were purified out of the Church and the pure Word of the Gospel was preached and imposed.

Other historians again look beyond the initial crisis, beyond the self-deceptions and conservative reflexes of most of those who went to war in 1642, to the dramatic events that followed the Parliamentarian victory in the first Civil War that raged from 1642 to 1646. They place the critical period after the fighting was over. This was after all a country in which it was extremely rare (perhaps only at a handful of county elections every few years) for more than 1,000 people to gather in one place at the same time. Yet there was now a war which saw armies of more than 10,000 criss-cross all but a few counties in each campaigning season, and in which the number of battle-dead after at least ten engagements exceeded the size of the crowds at all but the most populous of those county hustings. It was also a war in which the cost of sustaining more than one in ten of the adult male population in arms imposed terrible burdens on the working population. The victors in battle, finding that they could not win the peace, and finding the resentment of the uncommitted majority welling up against them, were to fall out amongst themselves, until one group with the naked military power to effect their will, determined to challenge the most basic institutions and values of their society and culture: they were to slaughter their King, abolish the monarchy and strip away the political and social privileges of the peerage.

To go with this levelling in the state went a levelling in the Church, with the abolition of bishops and the ending of the legal requirement on all Englishmen to attend their parish church every Sunday. By 1647, indeed, powerful groups in Parliament's victorious New Model Army and in the city of London were calling for the dissolution of all existing constitutional forms and for an entirely new 'Agreement of the People', a formal contract by which all those who wished to enjoy civil liberties bound themselves together to honour a paper constitution

9

Charles I, equipped for war, once he had been driven from his capital.

establishing a radically decentralized and democratized form of government strictly answerable to the people for the exercise of power. This demolition of the skyscrapers that had dominated the English skyline and this blueprint for a brave new world appeared to presage the creation of a new, libertarian (and in the aspirations of some, egalitarian) political, social and religious order. Although it was not to be, these mighty events have seemed to many historians to parallel the slaughter of kings, the abolition of monarchy, the assault on inherited wealth and prescriptive privilege, and the challenge to organized religion, that constitute the essence of the other great turmoils of Western Civilization which are unhesitatingly accorded the accolade of Revolutions.

This book does not seek to investigate those most-studied of all conundrums of English and of British history, the collapse of Charles's authority in 1637–41 and the taking up of arms in England in 1642. Just one point needs to be brought out here. It is increasingly clear that any account of the origins and nature of the conflict which concentrates exclusively on England is manifestly inadequate. The crises which overwhelmed the monarchies of Charles I in the years in and after

Cromwell, as Lord Lieutenant of Ireland in 1649. Notice how closely modelled this engraving is upon the previous picture of Charles I.

1638 were interrelated, and events in each kingdom affected what happened in the others. It was not the recall of the English Parliament which destabilized Charles's hold on England; it was the circumstances of that recall in the autumn of 1640 – with Charles militarily defeated, and with the Scots in effective control of the North-East of England and refusing to return home without reparations from an English Parliament – that made political confrontation possible. Yet the Scots rebelled against Charles for pursuing authoritarian policies kindred to those he followed in England.

Similarly, the timing of the Irish rebellion was catastrophically wrong for Charles. A rebellion six months earlier, in which thousands of Protestants were slaughtered, would have allowed the King to gain control of an army of conquest (the Houses would not have had the administrative assurance to demand control of it). If Charles had kept his nerve and continued to pursue (however insincerely) the conciliatory policies that he pursued in the autumn of 1641, fear of the 'many-headed monster' (the 'people', and especially religious separatists amongst the people) would have allowed Charles to regain a natural majority

11

Driuinge Men Women & children by hund:
reds vpon Briges & casting them into Riuers,
who drowned not were killed with poles &
shot with muskets.

*O*ne of the many horrific images of the massacre of Irish Protestants
published in England in 1641/2.

amongst the members of both Houses of Parliament: then, in the event of an Irish Rebellion six months later, Charles would again have secured control of the army of reconquest.

Any account of the dynamics of the Civil War would also need to look at the interpenetration of the wars in England, Ireland and Scotland: the Scots invasion of England to assist Parliament against the King in 1644 and the King against the Long Parliament in 1648; the Irish troops who destabilized Covenanting control of Scotland in 1645; the English and Scots who fought each other as well as fighting those Irish soldiers not fighting other Irish. Yet if any complete account must explore the *British* experience of conflict in the 1640s, it is legitimate to ask some questions which are particular to just one of the three kingdoms. Although soldiers from all three kingdoms fought in each of the Civil Wars, they remain three separate wars with their own codes, dynamics and outcomes. The *impact* of the war was very different for the inhabitants of each. Given the limitations of space in this book, it has therefore been decided to restrict it to the events in England and how they explain the outcome in England. What needs to be explained is how we get from the cautious and hesitant war aims of 1642 to regicide, a denouement willed exclusively in England without reference to the other kingdoms.

This book looks, then, at the *impact* of the Civil War in England in the 1640s. It does not concern itself with the origins of the War, why it broke out when it did, or why particular individuals or groups lined up as they did, in 1640 or in 1642. These complex questions have been extensively explored in other publications. Instead, the book looks at the functional radicalism of war, at the inexorable and grim logic of a war which saw families, local communities, the nation at large, divided against itself.

In chapter one, which follows this introduction, Charles Carlton examines the English Civil War as a military experience. He offers a graphic account of what it was like to be sucked into the formidable military machines created by both sides; of what it was like to be engaged in campaigning, to be on a seventeenth-century battlefield or in a seventeenth-century siege; and of how the civilian population became caught up in the cross-fire. And he offers a chilling estimate of the casualties of the fighting.

In chapter two, David Smith examines the search for a political settlement in the 1640s. He identifies the stress fractures in the ideology of the political élite, examines how the reforms of 1641–2 satisfied some but not others at Westminster and in the provinces, and explains how this led into a war which few wanted. He identifies three separate constitutional revolutions over the decade: the first, in 1641–2, witnessed change *with* the King's consent; a second, in 1642–7, imposed limitations on the Crown *without* the King's assent; and a third, in 1648–9, saw the outright abolition of monarchy. This chapter is notable for its careful analysis of the various peace proposals put forward at crucial stages in the unfolding drama.

Chapter three looks at the religious dynamics of the 1640s. The chapter opens by suggesting that religious opinions were especially sharply polarized at the outbreak of the wars. Behind the King stood those who were determined to preserve the heart of the Elizabethan Church settlement, the distinctive blend of Protestant theology within a traditional framework of Church government, and forms of worship that combined elements of reformed and traditional Catholic practice. Behind the Parliament stood men certain only of the need to purify the Church of its popish, idolatrous and superstitious elements and to construct a new Church purer to the commands of the Scriptures, and drawn much more narrowly from them. The chapter then explores the frustrations of Puritan activists in the 1640s, as the strength and resilience of 'parish Anglicanism' and as the inability of the godly to agree what that new purer Church should be like brought about the gradual disintegration of what had never been more than an amorphous coalition.

In chapter four Glenn Burgess takes up themes from the previous chapters. He looks at the impact on political thought, and examines the extraordinary outburst of pamphlets and tracts in which were explored fundamental questions about the nature of political authority and the rights of subjects to protect themselves from tyrannical governors. The chapter discusses in detail three of the most extensive debates of the decade: first, the debates about how far subjects might resist a badly-counselled King and about how to ensure that royal power was employed rightly; second, the attempt on all sides to articulate a theory of 'balance' or 'moderation'; and third, the debate about the responsibility of the civil governor to preside over the implementation of a programme of 'godly reform'. Chapters two to four therefore form a unity, and complement one another. They trace the way the realities of a country torn apart by war caused old assumptions and old certainties to dissolve, and new and frightening possibilities to take shape. One of the points on which all three authors of those chapters would agree is that support for the trial and execution of the King in the winter of 1648–9 was extremely

Major Civil War Battles and Sieges

22 Aug. 1642	King raises his standard
23 Oct. 1642	King (just) wins opening battle of EDGEHILL
12 Nov. 1642	Rupert storms and takes BRENTFORD
13 Nov. 1642	King retreats to winter quarters in Reading
19 Jan. 1643	Cornwall secured for King at battle of BRADDOCK DOWN
25 Apr. 1643	Earl of Essex captures READING
29 Jun. 1643	Royalists control Yorks after battle of ADWALTON MOOR
5–13 Jul. 1643	Royalist victories in West (LANSDOWN [Bath] and ROUNDWAY DOWN [Devizes])
26 Jul. 1643	Royalists capture BRISTOL
10 Aug.–5 Sep. 1643	Failed royal siege of Gloucester
20 Sep. 1643	Indecisive first battle of NEWBURY. Turning point of war
25 Sep. 1643	Anglo-Scots Solemn League and Covenant agreed
19 Jan. 1644	Scots army invades England
25 Jan. 1644	Royalist Protestant army from Ireland defeated at battle of NANTWICH (Cheshire)
21 Mar. 1644	Royalists raise siege of Newark
29 Mar. 1644	Waller defeats Royalists at battle of CHERITON (Surrey)
29 Jun. 1644	King defeats Waller at battle of CROPREDY BRIDGE (Oxon)

limited. In particular, support for these actions outside the New Model Army was astonishingly limited. Probably no more than one in ten of the MPs entitled to sit in the Long Parliament, before the Army purged it by arresting some members and turning many more away in December 1648, actively supported the King's trial and execution; and less than half the forty-three or so who did had been amongst those elected in peacetime conditions in 1640 (the rest were returned at by-elections in the mid-1640s, often as Army nominees). It is unlikely that the proportion of Parliamentarian supporters in the country as a whole who backed this denouement was any greater. Why then did the leadership in the Army use their naked military power to bring it about? This is the question that Ian Gentles sets out to answer in chapter five. He tells the story of that Army from its inception in the bleak midwinter of 1644–5 to what Oliver Cromwell is reputed to have called the 'cruel necessity' of the regicide.

At one level, as several of the chapters make clear, the Civil War was an old-fashioned struggle for power amongst the élite. The Parliamentarian cause can be plausibly seen as an attempted *coup d'état* by members of the ancient nobility, who saw themselves as the King's natural advisers (*consiliarii nati*). But it was more than that. It was also the first major rebellion in English

2 Jul. 1644	Three Parliamentarian armies defeat two Royalist armies at battle of MARSTON MOOR leading to surrender of York
21 Jul.–3 Aug. 1644	King defeats Earl of Essex at LOSTWITHIEL
27 Oct. 1644	Inconclusive second battle of NEWBURY
19 Dec. 1644	Self-Denying Ordinance in Parliament
April 1645	Formation of the New Model Army
30 May 1645	Rupert sacks LEICESTER
14 Jun. 1645	Royalists crushed at battle of NASEBY (Northants)
17 Jun. 1645	Fairfax retakes LEICESTER
10 Jul. 1645	New Model defeats Western Royalists at battle of LANGPORT
10 Sep. 1645	Fairfax takes BRISTOL
24 Sep. 1645	King defeated at battle of ROWTON MOOR (Chester)
30 Jan. 1646	Surrender of CHESTER
21 Mar. 1646	Last Royalist army surrenders at STOW-ON-THE-WOLD
5 May 1646	King surrenders to Scots
25 Jun. 1646	Surrender of OXFORD
March 1648	Revolt in South Wales
April 1648	Royalist revolt in the North and seizure of Berwick
May 1648	Revolt in Kent
May–Jul. 1648	Siege of PEMBROKE
Jun.–Aug. 1648	Siege of COLCHESTER
2 Aug. 1648	Cromwell defeats Scots Army at battle of PRESTON and invades Scotland

history in which many men and women throughout English society were making independent political choices. And as the élite squabbled, fought their private fights, gave examples of disobedience to those below them in society, so those below them determined to 'take advantage of the times, lest the like come not again'. In chapter six, John Walter looks at social tensions in the 1640s, and at the myths and realities of popular action and insurrection over the decade. He pays especial attention to the way the sources, especially those fed by gentry neurosis about the people as 'a many-headed monster', inflated the prospects for a 'revolution within a revolution'. He is then able to offer a sympathetic analysis of the spontaneous and variegated forms of popular action in town, countryside and parish church, and of how changes in the demands of the state and in its agencies created new challenges and new opportunities for participation in government for those who had hitherto been 'the governed'.

All the authors have drawn on the extraordinary explosion of pamphleteering and 'cheap print' in the 1640s. The illustrations in this book are drawn from this material too, reminding us that long before the invention of photography, visual images were making their own impact on that greater part of the population with access to pamphlets, (weekly) newspapers and tracts. In the final chapter, Peter

A vivid representation of the trial of Charles I, January 1649.

Thomas looks specifically at the impact of a decade of civil war and rebellion on the printed word. He chronicles the explosion of output; he examines the evolution of new and the adaptation of old literary forms, and he evokes the uses made of 'teeming liberty'. Some of the great names of English literature – Milton, Marvell, Herrick – have to jostle for space with the tabloid journalists telling their perennial tales of rapine and slaughter. It is an appropriate way to encapsulate a decade in which the barriers came down and Englishmen, in seeking to cope with a mild tyranny, brought themselves to the edge of chaos.

CHAPTER I

The Impact of the Fighting

CHARLES CARLTON

'My Dear and loving husband, my king love,' Susan Rodway began a letter of 1644 to Robert, a private in the London Trained Bands, who was away fighting at the siege of Basing House. Susan was worried about the lack of news from her husband, particularly as neighbours had received letters from theirs. She was concerned for her child: 'My little Willie has been sick this fortnight.' She missed her man desperately: 'You do not consider that I am a lone woman,' she reproved, 'I thought you would never leave me this long together.' But above all, Susan Rodway was terrified that her husband would be killed, and she would be left a widow, because she ended her letter 'So I rest ever praying for your safe return.'

Susan Rodway knew only too well something which can easily be forgotten both by historians as they fight over the causes and nature of the Civil Wars, and by enthusiasts as they dress up to re-enact battle on summer afternoons. Whatever the Civil Wars which engulfed the British Isles in the middle of the seventeenth century were – a Great Rebellion, a Puritan or Bourgeois Revolution, crises of liberty or of parliaments, wars of religion or of three kingdoms – of one thing there can be no doubt. As the American Civil War general, William T. Sherman, brutally put it: 'Men go to war to kill and get killed, and should expect no tenderness.'

It is extremely difficult to get some idea of the extent and experience of death in any holocaust, even when we have accurate statistics. For instance, the official tally of 765,399 British dead in the First World War does not convey the loss of a whole generation as powerfully as a name-crowded war memorial on some village green. Had the inhabitants of the parish of Myddle in Shropshire decided to build a memorial to their men who fought in the Civil War they would have carved 21 names into the stone, 13 of whom did not return – a higher proportion for the village than in the First World War. Six of them, including Thomas Formaston, 'a very hopeful young man', disappeared without trace. Richard Chalmer died at Edgehill, while Reece Vaughan and John Arthur perished storming Hopton Castle. Thomas Taylor was killed at Oswestry. After being shot by a comrade during a dispute over plunder, Nat Owen could not move and was burned alive when the Parliamentary army set fire to Bridgwater. Thomas and William Preece died fighting at Ercall, while their brother perished at the end of a rope, hanged for horse stealing.

Contemporaries tried to estimate the number of casualties taken during the Civil Wars. After the fighting was over, Thomas Hobbes reckoned that some 100,000 Englishmen had perished, while Sir William Petty put the figure at 300,000.

These estimates are, of course, inspired guesses. At the best of times early modern British statistics were rudimentary: war made their collection even more difficult. Tricks of memory, as well as the ploys of propagandists produced wildly different estimates. For instance, in the 19 contemporary accounts of the assault on St Mary's Tower during the Siege of York on 15 June 1644, casualties estimates range from about 20 to over 300.

During the Civil Wars in England some 635 incidents – ranging from Marston Moor, the Wars' bloodiest battle, to a fracas in Doncaster, where one man was stabbed – have been found, and estimates made of the killed and prisoners. They show the following:

	Killed	*Prisoner*
Parliament	34,141	34,493
Royalist	50,597	83,041
Total	84,738	117,534

Usually we think of the Civil Wars in terms of large battles or sieges in which thousands of men perished and crucial territory was lost or gained. In fact, most of the lives were not lost in these massive confrontations. Only 17 per cent of the Roundheads and 12 per cent of the Cavaliers died in the wars' nine major battles of over 1,000 casualties. On the other hand, 47 per cent on both sides perished in skirmishes of less than 200 dead.

The violence of war. A contemporary image.

Atrocities

On Christmas Day 1643 Lord Byron accepted the surrender of some 20 Parliamentarians at Barthomley, Cheshire. 'I put them all to the sword,' the Royalist commander boasted, 'which I find the best way to proceed with these kind of people.' Like all civil wars, the English Civil War was stained by atrocities.

Perhaps the War's most cold-blooded massacre occurred in February 1644, when Colonel Samuel Moor surrendered Holt Castle, Denbighshire. After their commander was marched off to be interrogated, his troops were murdered and their bodies were tossed into the moat. The Royalist sack of Bolton in May 1644 was the war's most serious authorized massacre. After the Puritan defenders hanged an Irish soldier from their walls to celebrate beating back an assault in which the Royalists lost some 300 men, Prince Rupert ordered Colonel Broughton's regiment to take the city – which they did, killing all the enemy, soldiers and civilians, they could find. Estimates of those killed range from between 200 to 1,800.

None the less, compared to modern civil wars there were remarkably few atrocities in England. Only three or four instances of the use of torture to interrogate prisoners have been found: burning match cord was inserted between the fingers of boys suspected of smuggling messages into besieged garrisons. Rape, which as the Russian Army demonstrated in 1945 is not a crime of sexual passion, but the ultimate act of violence against a despised enemy, was almost as rare. In May 1645 Captain Richard Symonds watched a soldier receive a lash from every carter in the baggage train for ravishing two women. Sir Samuel Luke, a reliable source, reported that during the spring of 1645 Sir Marmaduke Langdale's Cavaliers plundered and raped without mercy in Northamptonshire. Lord General Fairfax explained the violation of a farmer's wife before her husband at Otley, Yorkshire, by adding that the perpetrators were French.

The comparative absence of atrocities during the first English Civil War was due to the fact that both sides spoke the same language, and did not regard the other as inhuman malignants. Unhappily when ethnic or religious differences prevailed, as in Scotland and Ireland, or when Irish soldiers were captured fighting outside their native land, things were far less civilized.

In addition to deliberate killing on the field of battle, many soldiers lost their lives accidentally. This is not surprising, for weapons are inherently dangerous machines, especially in the hands of ill-trained troops or careless conscripts. The daily accidents became so serious that a Royalist officer complained that 'We bury more toes and fingers than we do men.'

Before technological advances in medicine, public health and the mass slaughter of the First World War, more soldiers died of war-related disease than from combat itself. The reasons were simple. From the crowded Royalist headquarters of Oxford, Lady Anne Fanshawe wrote that 'the sad spectacles of war', plague and sickness, came 'by reason of so many people being packed together'. During the summer of 1643, half the 6,000 Roundheads besieging Reading were too ill for duty. In winter, conditions got worse. 'Our lying in the field hath lost us more than have been taken away either by the sword or the bullet,' reported Captain Rich of the Essex levies in late October 1642.

Tiredness, hunger, contaminated food and water, long marches by day, and cold, broken sleep by night, all helped the spread of disease. Between 22 June 1647 and 20 April 1648 2,099 people died of the plague in war-torn Chester. War-related plague so devastated Stafford that it took a generation for its population to recover. Between July and September 1645 there was not a single christening in Manchester's parish church: they were too busy burying 748 corpses, a 40-fold increase over pre-war rates. Indeed so virulent was the plague there that many folk vowed that 'they would rather be hanged at their own door than enter such an infected town'.

Estimates of the ratio between the direct and indirect deaths from war in the seventeenth century vary. Jacques Dupaqurer, a French demographer, estimated that combat produced only 10 per cent of all fatalities. Geoffrey Parker puts this figure at 25 per cent. Between 1642–5 the annual death rate for the Banbury garrisons averaged 10 per cent, while that in more crowded cities such as Oxford, Bristol or Exeter, could well have been twice or even three times as high. Disease became particularly lethal during sieges. Joseph Bamfield, the Royalist governor of Arundel, attributed the majority of the 500 deaths of its 900-strong garrison during the siege to 'the bloody flux and spotted fever' – typhoid and diarrhoea. Archaeological findings support this view. An analysis of nine members of the Royalist garrison who were buried in the same grave during the siege of Sandal Castle, Yorkshire, shows that three of them died from metal wounds, such as shrapnel. One had a broken arm, two had blows to the head, while four show no skeletal damage, suggesting that they died from disease. Thus it would not be unreasonable to assume that the Civil Wars produced slightly more indirect deaths than direct ones.

In sum we might total casualties as follows:

Direct deaths from combat	84,738
Indirect deaths (i.e. disease)	100,000
Accidents	300
Bishop's Wars	500
Total	185,538

Of course this estimate is extremely rough, and to err once more on the side of caution it could be rounded down to say 180,000. This would mean that of England's population of roughly five millions, 3·6 per cent perished as a result of the civil wars. By comparison 2·6 per cent of the population of the United Kingdom lost their lives as a result of the First World War, and only 0·6 from the Second World War. The fact that the Civil Wars of the seventeenth century should have been the bloodiest conflict in relative terms in English history should not be surprising. After all the casualties on both sides were compatriots.

Statistics about death and dying do not, of course, convey what the experience of war was like for those who had to fight. For most seventeenth-century soldiers the impact of combat came in three main areas: first, the campaigns and low-level skirmishes that usually took place during the summer: second, the set-piece battles that were short and very sharp shocks in which each side tried to force a resolution: and finally during sieges, wherein some of the most brutal, and certainly the most prolonged fighting occurred.

Although campaigning armies moved very slowly (the average distance Chaplain Sprigge's regiment covered each day during the Naseby campaign of 1645 was eight miles), soldiers were constantly on the move, and being exposed to fairly high levels of violence. For instance, General William Waller's Parliamentary infantry marched on 36 of the 69 days between 23 May and 31 July 1644, staying no longer than three nights in one place. During an appallingly wet summer, they slept out in the open without even the cover of tents or bivouacs on 21 of those nights. During the 1644 Scots' invasion of England, Robert Douglas, a Covenanter, marched on 73 days and was involved directly or indirectly in 30 actions. He also heard 35 sermons. Between May and August of the same year George Hancock, a company clerk in the Parliamentary forces, took part in nine actions, including the capture of York and the Battle of Marston Moor. After Lieutenant Elias Archer left London with the trained bands on 16 October 1644 he was constantly on the move, and was involved in two skirmishes, a couple of false alarms, the hanging of deserters on two separate occasions, as well as four very ferocious assaults on Basing House. 'There did hardly one week pass,' Captain Atkyns recalled his experiences near Farnham at this time, 'in which there was not a battle or skirmish fought, or a beating up.'

Such short sudden blitzes could be quite terrifying. On the night of 25 June 1643 Colonel John Hurry's regiment overran a couple of hundred Roundheads whom they caught quite literally napping near West Wickham. A Cavalier crowed "Twas the terriblest thing in the world to have an Enemy fall unto one's quarters by night, and nothing more resembles the last resurrection and judgment than to see so many people rise up together naked.' Only the best troops could survive such a surprise. 'They fell up our rear before we could begin to march,' the Parliamentarian Luke Lloyd wrote home to his wife in June 1644, days after a skirmish at Tipton Heath. 'They assaulted us a quarter of a mile this side of the leager [overnight camp] with such fury that had not our men behaved themselves very gallantly we would have been utterly defeated.'

After Waterloo the Duke of Wellington observed that, 'The History of a battle is not unlike the history of a ball! Some individuals may recollect all the little events of which the great result is the battle lost or won: but no individual can recollect the order in which, or the exact moment at which they occurred.' Sir Richard Bulstrode came to the same conclusion when he tried to make sense of his own experiences at Edgehill:

> There is always great difference in relations of battles, it is certain that in a battle, the next man can hardly make a true relation of the actions of him that is next to him; for in such a Hurry and smoke of a Set Field, a man takes notice of nothing but what relates to his own safety. So that no man can give a clear account of particular passages.

The 'hedgehogs' of pikemen at the battle of Edgehill,
October 1642.

In many respects Civil War battles were a process in which united groups of men clashed, and started to break down into smaller units, and these ultimately became pockets of individuals. Confrontations could be between the same arms, such as infantry against infantry, or cavalry fighting cavalry, or between arms, when horsemen charged foot soldiers. Such mêlées were barely controlled disasters, for they were both confused and terrifying. Increasingly as time passed they limited the horizons of the participants, and became all the more a matter of individual survival. Once two sides had joined in the hurly-burly of hand-to-hand fighting, the battle field degenerated into huddles of densely crowded groups of milling men. Frightened humans tend to bunch; it is part of our herd instinct. Soldiers could become so pressed together that they could not fall down; even if wounded, the scrum carried them to and fro like broken flotsam as it heaved and hacked. Hemmed in by friend and foe most could not escape the crowd as it flowed hither and thither (a little like football fans up and down the terraces), threatening all the time to trample them under foot. Victory went to the group which destroyed the integrity of its opponents, thus turning a unit into a crowd. And when that took place, the killing of one man by another began in bloody earnest.

Billowing gunpowder smoke, whose acrid sulphuric smell assaulted nose and eyes, did much to reduce men's visibility, especially as fighting became more intense. Smoke was such a problem that armies would manoeuvre to get up wind of each other. The Royalists tried to do so at Marston Moor and Naseby. After Parliamentary efforts failed at Rowton Heath, a chaplain consoled himself with the thought that while 'they had the Wind and Sun, we had God with us'. Smoke plays tricks upon the eyes. Sometimes all a man could see was a dirty white bank penetrated by flashes of yellow and red, from which lines of the enemy would suddenly emerge, seeming against the billowing background to be taller and more intimidating.

Smoke was not the only thing to reduce a soldier's radius of visibility. If he were an infantry man he would be drawn up in a file one to two dozen men long, and perhaps as many as six deep. His helmet and weapon (especially a pike) limited his vision by making it hard to turn to see what was going on beside and behind him. The spatial reference points a soldier used were rarely topographical features – which explains why it is sometimes hard to say for sure where a battle actually took place. During the recent debate over the building of a motorway at Naseby, leading authorities differed by as much as half a mile over the battle's location. At the time soldiers defined their place in combat by reference to the colours their units carried to show them where they were and where they should be. Leaders sometimes fulfilled a similar role. Towards the end of the Second Battle of Newbury Sir Charles Lucas threw off his protective buff coat so that his own regiment (as well as enemy sharp shooters) could see his white shirt in the dusk.

If a soldier's radius of visibility in battle was limited, so too were the threats to his survival, particularly when the immediate press of the enemy gave musketeers no time to reload. As men swung musket butts, and slashed with their swords, they could only kill or be killed at arm's length.

Close order combat varied depending on whether it took place between infantry and cavalry, or between similarly armed groups.

For instance, when infantry attacked infantry, one line would tend to stand their ground as the other advanced. Each would fire one volley, perhaps two if they had time, before colliding with each other. 'We came after our shot was spent to push of pike, and fought very gallantly having no relief from our horse,' recalled Lord Belasyse of Edgehill. Sir William Brereton described what it was like to stand and receive the enemy. At Rowton Heath they attacked, 'with great resolution and boldness, and in very good order', and they 'fought so long and so fiercely until all their powder and bullet was spent. Afterwards they joined and fell to it pell-mell, one upon the other, with the stocks of their muskets.'

This process, which was known as coming 'to push of pike' rarely took place in such a dramatic fashion. Large bodies of pikemen, their weapons held out horizontally, rarely smashed into one another coldbloodedly, and if they did converge, chest armour, rounded helmets, face visors, and even buff coats deflected pike thrusts. Daniel Lupton, the veteran, thought that not one pikeman in 20 was resolute and strong enough to be able to stand his ground and use his 16-foot weapon skilfully enough to damage the enemy in such a confrontation. Contact was usually made in the fashion that Sir Walter Slingsby saw at Cheriton: 'The foot, keeping their ground in a close body, not firing till

*F*rom a military training manual
(1644).

within two pikes length [32 feet], and then three ranks at a time, after turning the butt end of their muskets, charging the pikes, and standing close, preserved themselves, and slew many of the enemy.'

Contact between cavalry and cavalry was similar. According to military manuals, horse soldiers were expected to charge *en masse*, as close to each other as possible, with each man's knee tucked behind that of the man to his right. In practice cavalry did not gallop straight into enemy lines, for no matter how fiercely spurred, at the last moment horses will stop, or shy away. Rather they rode up to the other side, fired their pistols or carbines, before retiring to reload. Only after the enemy lines started to disintegrate would the cavalry join in hand-to-hand combat. Lord Bernard described how this process took place at Edgehill: 'We were fain to charge them uphill and leap over some five or six hedges and ditches, they gave fire with the canon lined among their horse, dragoons, carbines and pistols, but finding nothing did dismay the king's horse . . . when our men charged, they all began to turn head, and we followed an execution upon them four or five miles together.'

In these two instances the defending cavalry broke and ran just before the attacking troops arrived at their position. When they stood their ground, a mêlée of hand-to-hand fighting followed. At Marston Moor: 'The Horse on both sides behaved themselves with the utmost bravery; for having discharged their pistols, and flung them at each other, they fell to it with their swords.' At Rowton Heath: 'After pistols were discharged at half pike's distance [i.e. eight feet, point blank range] they disputed the matter with their swords for a full quarter of an hour, neither giving ground to another, till at length the enemy were forced to retreat.'

So long as they did not break ranks, infantry were comparatively safe from cavalry attacks. Horses will not run into fixed objects, whether they are walls of men or of stone. Infantry could make the former more formidable by lining them with pikes, or by having musketeers pound metal-tipped stakes, known as 'swines' feathers', into the ground before them at an angle which pointed to the enemy.

In both battles and skirmishes, it was not the impact of charging cavalry, but the sight of their fearsome approach that broke infantry, particularly poorly trained recruits. At Edgehill Captain Nathaniel Fiennes saw 'Four other regiments ran away, and fought not at all, but cast away their colours', when Prince Rupert's cavalry advanced towards them. The only time horse soldiers could expect to break resolute infantry was when they suddenly attacked the rear or flanks of tired men already engaged in fighting other infantry. Such was the secret of the victory that Cromwell's Ironsides won both at Marston Moor and Naseby.

There is no doubt that artillery badly frightened Civil War soldiers. With their dreadful weapons, convoluted jargon of sakers, minions, and drakes and culverins, and complicated mathematical formulae, gunners were seen as a mystery that practised well-nigh satanic arts. 'The first shot for the devil,' ran an artillery axiom, 'the second for God, and the third for the King.' 'From the Devil's arse did guns beget,' wrote Ben Jonson, the soldier turned playwright. John Milton agreed, calling cannon 'a devilish machination to plague the Sons of men.' Colonel Slingsby, whose intimacy with artillery was closer than the poet's,

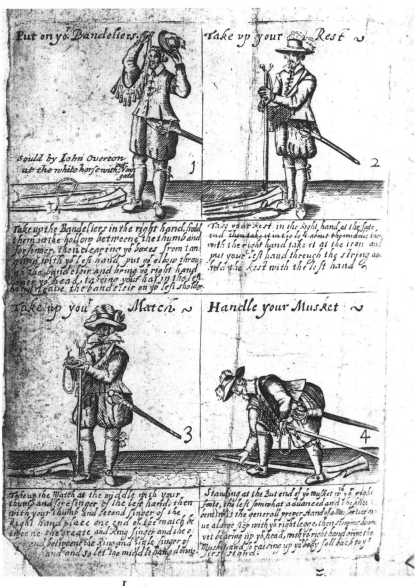

*L*oading a musket. From a training manual.

saw 'legs and arms flying apace' when cannon fired point blank at infantry. At the First Battle of Newbury Captain Gwynn witnessed 'A whole file of men, six deep, with their heads struck off with one cannon shot of ours.' Sergeant Henry Foster, another Roundhead, remembered that it was 'somewhat dreadful when bowels and brains flew in our faces'.

The climax of Civil War battles came with the disintegration of enemy units into crowds of milling individuals, a phase which contemporaries called 'a panic

Women and the War

Civil War made life for seventeenth-century English women even more difficult than it was in peace.

Some women died in the fighting, either through accidents or as civilian bystanders particularly during sieges, or as camp followers who got caught up in hostilities. A few brave females, such as Charlotte, Countess of Derby, Lady Mary Bankes, and Lady Brilliana Harley, defended their husbands' castles with the ferocity of lionesses protecting their lairs. A handful of women even dressed and fought as men. Jane Engleby, the daughter of a Yorkshire yeoman, is said to have charged with the King's cavalry at Marston Moor, and wounded, escaped back to the security of her father's farm.

While their husbands were away fighting, or were abroad, many women took over the administration of estates or the running of workshops. Some, like Lady Mary Verney, undertook the arduous task of negotiating with Parliamentary committees for the return of confiscated (or sequestered) lands. This involved lengthy debates about the value and yield of the estates and the rate of fine to be paid for their recovery.

Indeed for most women the Civil War was a disruption of their normal lives. It broke up families. A year after his marriage, Basil Fielding went off to fight for the King. His wife, Elizabeth, sent him a stream of nigh-hysterical letters. 'You cannot imagine what I would give to see you again,' she wrote in one, adding in another, 'Oh dear God, what I would give to see you, for God's sake write to me, and come as soon may be.' Husbands or fathers could be killed, leaving wives behind to bring up children. Uncertain if her husband had survived the rout of Charles II's forces at Worcester in 1650 'for three days', remembered Anne Fanshawe, 'I neither ate, nor slept, but trembled at every motion I heard, expecting the fatal news.' She was exceedingly relieved to learn that Sir Richard had been taken prisoner, and following him to London would stand outside his cell at dawn to talk.

War made pregnancy and childbirth all the more dangerous: many women miscarried or else had deformed babies. Forced to leave Oxford, the Queen, Henrietta Maria nearly died in Exeter giving birth to a daughter with one shoulder lower than the other. 'Here is the woefullest spectacle my eyes yet ever looked upon,' an attendant wrote 'the most worn and weak pitiful creature in the world, the poor Queen.'

fear'. According to an eyewitness of the collapse of the Parliamentary forces at Brentford, it took place when 'unnatural, shameful and strange cruelties send forth a voice . . . so loud and piercing that it awakes even secure and sleepy manhood'. Active soldiers described disintegration in more prosaic terms. Sir Bevil Grenville told his wife how the charge he led against the rebels at Braddock Down 'struck great terror in them, they stood not the first charge of foot, but fled in great disorder'. Holles' and Ballard's regiments displayed a similar lack of resolution at Edgehill. 'Upon the first charge of the enemy they wheeled about, abandoned their muskets, and came running down with the Enemy's horse at their heels and amongst them pell-mell.' James Lumsden noted 'those that fled were so possessed with a panic fear, that they ran.'

Veterans could sense when a unit was about to disintegrate, and would do all they could to prevent the catastrophe. At Powick Bridge, 'an old soldier' tried to rally the Parliamentary forces, but it was too late, and 'in the confused panic', they ran 'in a very dishonourable manner'. Recognizing at Naseby that his cavalry were about to break, the first of the fear-possessed men having already galloped past him, the King wanted to lead his reserves into the affray to stem the panic and win the day. But the War was not to have a Hollywood ending: Charles and Cromwell did not fight it out hand-to-hand. Grabbing his sovereign's bridle, the Earl of Carnwath shouted, 'will you go unto your death?' This gesture, combined with a confused order, backfired. Petrified, the Royalist reserves rode hell for leather back to Leicester, leaving the infantry to their fate.

In a crowded battlefield, disintegration did not take place at the front of a body of men. It could not. The rout began at the rear, where men could see and hear enough of the fighting to lose their nerve, and had enough room to run. Sometimes an attack, or the immediate threat of an attack from behind, would precipitate the collapse. Or else the erosion took place on the sides, where men were both exposed to enemy fire, and could still escape. Lord Belasyse described how this took place at Edgehill. After his troops had been fighting hand-to-hand with the enemy infantry for some time, Lord General Essex sent in the Parliamentary reserves who 'following upon our flank and charging through when we were at push of pike, we were at last broken'.

Once a unit started to break it had a rippling effect. Panic became contagious. 'Away! Away! Everyman shift for his Life', Sergeant Foster remembered the cry as his unit was ambushed near Aldermaston. At night, caught in a narrow lane, not just men, but animals panicked. Horses tried to bolt, overturning wagons, their loads blocking the thickly hedged road. A munitions wagon caught fire, blew up, killing ten men: it terrified the rest, and illuminated targets for the Royalist snipers in the hedges.

The sudden, accidental explosion of a powder wagon or magazine broke units during the Battles of Lansdown and Torrington. 'Truly, Sir, I never saw God in any part of my life,' a Parliamentary trooper told a friend about the explosion of 80 barrels of powder stored in Torrington parish church, which killed at least 200 men in a flash. The death of a leader at a critical moment could have a similar effect. The battle cries of troops confident of victory could shatter men whose cohesion was beginning to crumble. Hand-to-hand combat is extremely tiring, particularly for exhausted, frightened and hungry men, at the end of their tether, hardly amenable to reason or discipline. 'The frightened soldier, as well as the hungry belly, has no ears,' observed a certain Roger Boyle, a veteran of the Civil War.

Once men succumbed to fear the truly terrible time began. Sir Arthur Trevor, a survivor, recalled the horror of being routed at Marston Moor: 'In the fire, smoke and confusion of that day I knew not for my soul whither to incline. The runaways on both sides were so many, so breathless, so speechless, and so full of fears that I should not have taken them for men.' Only 100 of 2,000 infantry survived. A terrible blood lust made any rout even more ghastly. Perhaps it sprang from some basic human instinct rooted in our prehistory, when as hunters men ran down and slaughtered defenceless game – the helplessness of victims further arousing their frenzy.

Several incidents after Nazeby demonstrated this process. Having broken through the King's lines the Roundheads came across a party of women, whose faces they slashed, killing some. Missing the turn to Lubenham, a party of the King's horse rode down a cul-de-sac into Marston Trussell churchyard, in which, like cornered game, they were slaughtered to a man, their corpses being tossed into a clay pit. After running for 30 miles, a survivor tried to steal a loaf of bread from a farmhouse near Ravenstone. The soldier was so demoralized that a servant girl was able to kill him with the stick she was using to stir the laundry.

Physical circumstances made the wounds inflicted during pursuit far more lethal than those given in hand-to-hand combat. During the latter there were few stab wounds: instead men instinctively slashed at each other with swords, inflicting gory, yet superficial cuts. But in hot pursuit, when cavalry chased terrified foot soldiers, swords swung down, severing necks, or breaking backbones. After Sir John Digby's cavalry broke the Roundhead foot at Torrington in 1643 they chased them 'until their swords were blunted with the slaughter'. Two hundred were killed, and two hundred taken prisoner. The high ratio of dead to captured suggests that the Cavaliers went beserk in an orgy of butchery. Of the survivors, a contemporary recorded, there was 'scarce a man without a cut over the head or face'.

The Duke of Wellington observed that 'Nothing except a battle lost can be half so melancholy as a battle won.' And there could be no sadder scene than a field where brother had slain brother. A few days after the second battle of Newbury, a Royalist told a Parliamentary friend, 'the sight of so many brought to Oxford, some dead, some wounded, would make any true English heart bleed'. An observer of the same calamity agreed that 'It was a lamentable spectacle

Pikemen, marching to battle to the rhythm of fife and drum.

the next morning to behold what heaps of bodies and diversities of slaughters.' Initially they lay in a relaxed fashion, as if sleeping, their limbs entwined, their congealed blood mingled, a little like those sepia photographed corpses of the American Civil War. But after a few days, once *rigor mortis* had set in, and the dead had been stripped and tossed aside, they resembled the pathetically white matchsticks shown on films of liberated concentration camps.

Similar horrors could be seen after every major battle. At Edgehill 'the field was covered with the dead, yet no one could tell to what party they belonged'. At Naseby 'I saw the field so strewed with carcasses of horses and men,' a Roundhead wrote, 'the bodies lay slain about four miles in length, but most thick on the hill where the king stood.' Simeon Ashe recalled 'in the morning there was a mortifying object to behold, when the naked bodies of thousands lay upon the ground and not altogether dead.' What stunned one witness the most was the 'crying there was for surgeons as never was the like heard'.

Although each regiment was supposed to have a surgeon (equipped with a medicine chest costing 25 pounds), the lack of medical skills and knowledge meant that the plight of wounded survivors was appalling. Those who received immediate attention, either from trained medics or friends, had a better chance of surviving: thus after Edgehill the ratio of wounded to killed for officers was twice that of other ranks. But all too often there was little even the best medical men could do. 'Death,' confessed Edward Coke, a Parliamentary surgeon, 'will prevail.'

This process of combat building up to a climax, which suddenly broke into a tidal wave of killing, also took place during sieges. But then it was an unmitigated horror. Assaulting a fortified position was far more dangerous than attacking ranks of men drawn up on a battlefield. Going once more into the breach was a last desperate resort which usually resulted in filling up the walls with your own dead. Of a sample of 25 major Civil War sieges only two ended in a successful storm.

In the first place charging across open ground to reach a breach was a terrible ordeal. 'To adventure naked bodies against an Army defended with Stone-Walls, Strong-Works, and a Castle,' wryly noted an eyewitness of the parliamentary assault on Bristol of August 1645, 'was an argument of little self respect.' A similar point was made after the Roundhead assault on Derby: 'the enemies being in the works, nothing but their heads appearing, and the parliament's force being without defence in the open field.'

The Royalist veteran, Richard Atkyns, knew only too well the vulnerability of flesh and blood to lead and iron during a storm. He wrote, 'twould grieve one's heart, to see men drop like ripe fruit in a strong wind, and never see their enemy.' A defender used similar language to describe the failure of the parliamentary assault against Bolton on 28 May 1644. 'We gave them about half an hour's sharp entertainment . . . and repulsed them bravely to the enemy's great loss and discouragement, and in retreat cut them down before them in great abundance, and they fell like leaves from a tree in a winter storm.' No military action was bloodier and more brutal than a storm. A Roundhead warned Sir John Byron that if he wanted to take Nottingham Castle 'he must wade to it in blood.' Richard Sandys and his Roundheads took half an hour of bitter fighting 'at swords' point' before they reached the top of the defences at Shelford House. A fortnight later, on 21 November 1645, Sandys and his officers had to use their swords to drive their own men against the defences of Belvoir Castle, 'the strongest I have seen in England'. Afterwards the victors turned their weapons upon the enemy, slaughtering them without quarter and without exception.

Just as the critical moment in a battle took place when a unit disintegrated, in a siege it occurred when the defenders broke. But during a siege this collapse could be a far more terrible affair. Because it took longer to bring about, and because it was far harder to overcome troops hiding behind earthworks, as opposed to standing in open order, disintegration in a siege was all too often followed by a blood bath. From her experiences as the governor's wife during the siege of Nottingham, Lucy Hutchinson described this process: 'the brave turn cowards, fear unnerves the most mighty, makes the generous base, and great men do those things that they blush to think on.'

A Royalist recalled how the enemy fell apart when he stormed Cirencester in 1643: 'they were at their wits' end, and stood like men amazed, fear bereft them of understanding and memory.' While only a few defenders were killed in the storm itself, many were slain afterwards. One of the attackers recalled how the successful breach of Cardigan Castle's walls turned the defenders into 'men bereft of all sense'. They could not even fire the cannon loaded with grape already aimed at the breach, which would have repulsed the attack. Dropping their smoking linstocks, they craved for mercy: it was granted. Once the Scots breached Newcastle's defences Royalist resistance evaporated. Trapped in the market place, 'they presently called for quarter, and laying down their arms without assurances, some were taken, some were shaken, some stood still, and some fled away to hide the bleeding bodies in some secret shelter.' In May 1644, after the Parliamentarians crossed the outer wall, Lincoln's garrison collapsed equally precipitously. Taking to their heels, they ran not knowing which way to turn. One of the butchers recalled that they 'cried out for quarter, saying that they were poor Array men [conscripts]. We slew fifty of them.'

Ever since the walls came tumbling down at Jericho 4,500 years ago, victorious soldiers have believed that they were entitled to a sack after a storm. Because there were more psychological than economic rewards for the enduring of a storm, sacks were carried out with needless brutality. After watching Fairfax's troops violate Sherborne Castle in 1645 an observer noted that 'five shillings gotten in the way of spoil from the enemy gives them more content than twenty shillings by way of reward'.

If wages are the payment for work, then plunder is the perquisite of power. Soldiers, who are usually drawn from the bottom of society, and are always ordered about by those at the top, can themselves put the boot in, when there is an opportunity to plunder. In more ways than one, as they rampage through a captured city, still terrified by the sights and sounds of the storm they have barely survived, many victorious soldiers turn the world upside down. For the victims the upheaval is even more traumatic. 'Oh what a night and morning was that in which Bradford was taken,' recalled Joseph Lister, 'I was about twelve or thirteen years old, and though I was afraid of being killed, yet I was weary of so much fasting and praying.'

After losing 30 of their men in the breach the King's infantry were fighting mad

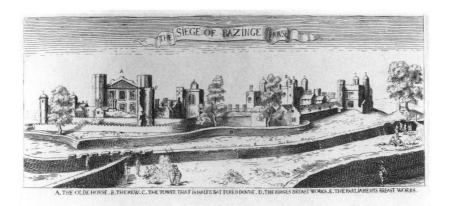

*The scene of one of the bloodiest encounters
in the Civil War.*

as they sacked Leicester in May 1645. They hanged Mr Raynor, 'an honest religious gentleman'. They killed Mr Sawyer in cold blood. They massacred many prisoners of war, and 'put diverse women inhumanly to the sword'. By nightfall, remembered Captain Richard Symonds, one of the attackers, there was 'scarce a cottage unplundered . . . and no quarter given to any in the heat'. Many of the assault troops were infantry from the poor mountainous counties of mid-Wales, who robbed with enthusiasm and without mercy. The parish registers, which show 709 burials immediately after the siege, do not tell the full story of the horror. Once a prosperous and happy citizen, William Summers not only lost his house, fruit trees, all his possessions, and his son, but his wife went mad with grief. He had to find work as a butcher.

In England there was no bloodier storm nor more vicious sack than that of Basing House in 1645. After weeks of artillery fire, 6,000 of Cromwell's troops attacked at six in the morning on 16 October. Once through the breach, 'the dispute was long and sharp, the enemy for aught I can learn, desired no quarter, and I believe had but little offered them.' Many, including women, perished in the hot blood of a final assault. A trooper smashed in the head of Dr Griffiths' daughter when she tried to protect her father. Some royalists, including six priests, were murdered in cold blood. 'Cursed be he that doth the Lord's Work negligently,' said Major Thomas Harrison, as he shot Major Robinson (who had been a Drury Lane comedian in civilian life). Harrison also killed Major Craffaud as he was trying to escape. 100 Cavaliers died, and three times as many were taken prisoner, as they were plundered without mercy.

After the smoke cleared, and the wounded were dragged off to the surgeons' knives, and the prisoners marched to the Tower, both vanquished and victors were grateful just to be alive. Many good men left their bones at Basing House. Robert Rodway was almost certainly one of them, perishing in the previous year's assault. And thus his widow, Susan, learned all too well the lesson that is so oft forgot – that men go to war to kill and be killed, and rarely receive any tenderness there.

CHAPTER II

The Impact on Government

DAVID L. SMITH

I

On 9 July 1642, Sir Benjamin Rudyerd, later a moderate Parliamentarian, warned the House of Commons not to demand further concessions from Charles I. Such demands would, he argued, be 'hazardous' and 'unsafe': Parliament should rest content with what it had already achieved for it could never 'make a mathematical security'. The history of English government during the 1640s can be written around this phrase. In constitutional terms, the Civil War was fought over the extent to which the King's prerogative and Parliament's privileges might be mathematically defined. It can be argued that the 1640s witnessed three distinct constitutional revolutions: those of 1640–1 (change *with* the King's consent); 1642–7 (change *without* the King's consent); and 1648–9 (the removal of the King completely). First, however, it is necessary briefly to explore the nature of the early Stuart constitution.

II

The English polity as it had developed by the early seventeenth century was both a 'personal monarchy' and a 'mixed monarchy'. England lacked a modern concept of the impersonal 'State', and retained many elements of personal rule from its medieval past: government, administration and justice were exercised in the monarch's name; the monarch was free to choose his/her own advisers, judges, military officers and higher clergy; and the royal Court was an important centre of political activity. Above all, the monarch wielded extensive discretionary powers known collectively as the royal 'prerogative'. These included the right to summon and dissolve Parliament at will; to declare war and conclude peace; and occasionally to pursue certain emergency policies in the interests of national security.

Yet many men believed that England was also a 'mixed monarchy', that monarchs had bound themselves and their successors to govern by consent. The polity combined the best aspects of hereditary monarchy with those of government by consent. The reforms of the 1530s enshrined this principle. Thereafter, the statutes enacted by the King-in-Parliament were clearly established as the highest form of law. By the early seventeenth century it was a commonplace that the natural relationship between Crown and subjects was one of harmony and symbiosis. This system, known to contemporaries as the 'ancient constitution', revolved around a monarchy which was both 'personal' and 'mixed'. England, it seemed, had managed to have its constitutional cake and eat it.

Unfortunately, this attractive ideal would disintegrate if the powers of either monarch or people were taken to their logical extreme. The locus of ultimate authority was never defined and there was no machinery for arbitration if Crown and Parliament quarrelled. The polity therefore depended for its smooth running on the maintenance of grey areas, of a delicate balance between royal and popular rights. This system *could* work, and did so satisfactorily in the 'Jacobethan' period. But it was acutely vulnerable to a change of monarch. A monarchy both 'personal' and 'mixed' would inevitably be destabilized if the monarch's personality did not 'mix' well with the political nation.

This was precisely what happened under Charles I. Charles used his agreed discretionary powers in ways which conflicted with the expectations and assumptions of many within the political élite. He raised financial levies (the Forced Loan in 1627, Ship Money from 1634–9) to avoid consultation with Parliament; he overruled the processes of the common law (as in the Five Knights' case); above all, he encouraged Laud's Church reforms which significantly narrowed the boundaries of legitimate religious belief. The King's personality contrasted sharply with those of his immediate predecessors. He was cold, aloof and inaccessible to his subjects, while his wish to define constitutional ambiguities was peculiarly dangerous in this system which rested on blurred distinctions. The eleven years during which Charles ruled without Parliament (1629–40) focused these grievances and encouraged fears of what John Pym called 'a design to alter the kingdom both in religion and government'. The instinctive reaction of critics like Pym was to blame this 'design' on the King's 'evil counsellors'. But during the 1640s a sickening fear gradually spread that Charles was himself implicated in the conspiracy. This posed a profound and wholly unforeseen question: how can the constitution be preserved if the monarch wishes to subvert it? It was this problem which led to the search for 'a mathematical security'.

III

When the Long Parliament assembled on 3 November 1640 MPs were unanimous in wanting to destroy the potential for another Personal Rule. They did not intend to *change* the constitution. Rather, they sought to restore a lost balance between royal powers and popular rights by punishing those 'evil counsellors' who had led the King astray, by removing the institutional apparatus of the Personal Rule, and by guaranteeing Parliament a permanent place in government. During the first nine months of the Long Parliament (November 1640–July 1641) this programme was systematically turned into legislation, *with the King's consent*. In practice, however, these measures, though born of the most conservative motives, imposed new limits on royal discretionary powers, especially those of summoning and dissolving Parliament at will. In sum, they marked the first of three constitutional revolutions during the 1640s.

Parliament dealt first with two of the King's most hated 'evil counsellors': Thomas Wentworth, Earl of Strafford, and Archbishop William Laud. In December 1640 Laud was impeached and imprisoned in the Tower pending a fuller trial. Articles of impeachment were likewise drawn up against Strafford in January 1641. But at his trial before the House of Lords, his enemies were unable to prove Strafford guilty of treason and they therefore resorted to a bill of attainder. This simply convicted Strafford of 'endeavouring to subvert the ancient and fundamental laws and government of His Majesty's realms of England and Ireland, and to introduce an arbitrary and tyrannical government against law in

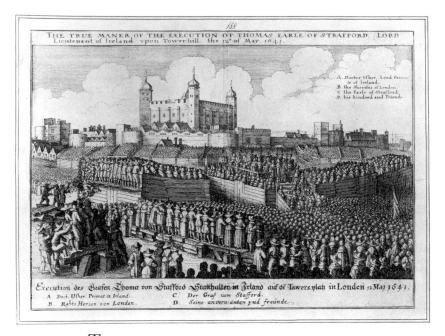

*T*he execution of Charles' feared minister, the Earl of Strafford,
12 May 1641.

the said kingdoms'. These words clearly show Parliament's intense concern to prevent subversion of the law and innovation in government. Intimidated by huge demonstrations outside Whitehall, the King broke his earlier promises and permitted Strafford's execution on 12 May 1641. Nor were Laud and Strafford isolated victims. By mid-1641, over half Charles's Privy Councillors of November 1640 were either imprisoned, exiled or disgraced. It was widely hoped that the King would now receive sound advice.

Parliament then turned from individuals to institutions. By far the most hated instruments of Charles's Personal Rule were the Courts of Star Chamber (the Privy Council acting as a court of law) and High Commission. The first had imposed harsh penalties on Charles's critics (Prynne, Burton, Bastwick, Lilburne, Leighton), while the second had enforced reforms in the Church and punished those who resisted. Both courts were abolished by statute on 5 July 1641. Once again, Parliament's obsessive desire to halt perceived innovation and to preserve the 'ancient constitution' was very striking. The 'act . . . for taking away the Court commonly called the Star Chamber' quoted *Magna Carta* and eight statutes passed between the reigns of Edward III and Henry VIII to prove that the Privy Council sitting as Star Chamber had 'of late times' acted 'contrary to the law of the land and the rights and privileges of the subject'. Similarly, Parliament claimed that High Commission had recently exercised 'other authority not belonging to [its] jurisdiction'. Once it was abolished, 'no new Court' was to be created with the 'like power, jurisdiction or authority' as High Commission 'pretendeth to have'. Thus by mid-1641 Parliament had not only removed the 'evil counsellors' who advised unpopular policies; it had also destroyed the means by which those policies were implemented.

But the most far-reaching step taken in 1640–1 was the guaranteeing of Parliament's role in government. Hitherto, Parliament had been, in Conrad Russell's words, 'an event rather than an institution'. It sat for short periods, at irregular intervals, and was summoned and dissolved entirely at the King's discretion. But after the Personal Rule few MPs trusted Charles to work with Parliament voluntarily and they therefore sought legislation binding him to do so. This consisted of two statutes: the Triennial Act (15 February 1641) which obliged Charles to call Parliament at least once every three years; and the 'act against the dissolving of the Long Parliament without its own consent' (11 May 1641). These acts limited the King's prerogative to summon and dissolve Parliament at will; and – like the attack on 'evil counsellors' and 'evil courts' – Charles assented to them.

The constitutional revolution of 1640–1 met with near-universal rejoicing in Parliament. Sir Benjamin Rudyerd called it 'a dream of happiness' and assumed that the troubles between Charles I and Parliaments would now be over. Yet only a year later the English Civil War broke out. This prompts us to ask whether the various measures of 1640–1 contained a formula for workable government. *Could* they have provided stability? The reforms were surely not *intrinsically* flawed. After all, they were never repealed, and in 1660–2 they formed the basis of the Restoration Settlement. Yet in the context of mid-1641 they failed. The problem was that Charles's critics had been almost *too* successful: they had destroyed the personnel and machinery of the Personal Rule; they had ensured Parliament's survival; and they had achieved all this with Charles's consent. If 'evil counsellors' really were responsible for royal policies that should have been enough. Having carried all before them, MPs now had no fall-back position. Thus, if the King continued to pursue unpopular policies, if his actions still threatened the rule of law and the 'arch of government', Parliament would have no choice but to devise more drastic solutions – solutions which would lead it into uncharted constitutional waters.

IV

This is precisely what happened. The failure of the constitutional measures of 1640–1 to produce stability was shown by the disintegration of the Parliamentary consensus which had designed them. Whereas in May only 59 MPs in a House of over 400 voted against Strafford's attainder, on 22 November the Grand Remonstrance (see below) was passed by a mere eleven votes (159 to 148). During the summer and autumn of 1641 an irreconcilable division opened within the political nation which culminated in civil war. To explain this split we must examine two closely connected subjects: the religious context, and the British context.

Nobody objected when Laud and thirteen like-minded bishops were impeached in December 1640. But when the Commons turned in the summer of 1641 to debate the future of episcopacy a fundamental disagreement emerged between those MPs who wished to preserve the office of bishop once the Laudians had been purged, and those who thought it an inherently corrupt office which should be abolished 'root-and-branch'. For men like Pym, 'further reformation' in the Church was an essential bulwark against the 'popish plot'. Many others, however, would have agreed with the future Royalist Edmund Waller when he called episcopacy 'the counterscarp and outwork of the whole social order'. Thus, while some MPs urged Charles to reform the Church, as many welcomed his refusal to do so. The constitutional revolution of 1640–1 had been achieved by a united Parliament; but when that unity collapsed over religious issues it could offer no remedy.

Events elsewhere in Britain deepened these divisions and heightened the sense of crisis. The 'Incident' of August 1641, when Charles tried to arrest his leading Scottish critics, showed that he was still prepared to use force to silence opposition. Even more serious, in October, Catholics in Ulster rebelled and massacred perhaps 3,000 Protestants. They claimed (almost certainly falsely) to be following the King's instructions. This apparently confirmed the existence of a 'popish plot' and presented a direct security threat to England. It posed a stark and utterly unprecedented question: could Charles be trusted to lead an army against the rebels? Hitherto, the King's right to command his own troops had been an undoubted part of his prerogative. But what if he were in league with the rebels, or so badly advised as to be unwilling to suppress them? What could Parliament do then to safeguard national security? Once again, *nothing* in the legislation of 1640–1 provided an answer to this problem.

Pym's attempted solution was presented in the Grand Remonstrance of November 1641. His diagnosis of England's ills was unchanged: 'the root of all [the] mischief' was 'a malignant and pernicious design of subverting the fundamental laws and principles of government upon which the religion and justice of this kingdom are firmly established'. The Remonstrance then catalogued instances of misgovernment since Charles became King (98 clauses) and described Parliament's earlier attempts to remedy these (65 clauses). However, the third section of 41 clauses contained two quite new demands, directly conditioned by the crises in religion and in Britain. The first was for 'a general synod of . . . divines' to 'consider of all things necessary for the peace and good government of the Church'. The second was that Charles 'employ such councillors, ambassadors, and other ministers in managing his business at home and abroad as the Parliament may have cause to confide in'. Charles received the Remonstrance on 1 December and replied three weeks later. Although he declared that a synod on Church affairs was unnecessary, he agreed to 'take it into consideration'. But he utterly refused to surrender 'the choice of . . . councillors and ministers of state', for that was 'the undoubted right of the Crown of England'. This showed that Parliament could no longer hope to secure the King's consent to its demands: if it sought further security, further controls on the King's behaviour, it would have to act *alone*.

It was therefore inevitable that a direct threat to its physical safety would drive Parliament to take radical constitutional steps. Charles I posed just such a threat on 4 January 1642 when, accompanied by an armed guard, he attempted to arrest one peer and five members of the Commons. Parliament responded with the Militia Ordinance. This blamed the 'late . . . most dangerous and desperate design upon the House of Commons' on 'the bloody counsels of papists and other ill-affected persons who have already raised a rebellion in the kingdom of Ireland'. To preserve 'the safety . . . of His Majesty's person, the Parliament and

Colonell Lunsford assaulting the Londoners at Westminster Hall, with a great rout of ruffinly Cavaleires

England dissolves into war, 1642.

kingdom in this time of imminent danger', the ordinance then nominated Lords Lieutenant whom both Houses trusted. The King insisted that he alone had the power to make such military appointments, and rejected the ordinance outright. On 5 March Parliament therefore took the unprecedented step of enacting the ordinance *on its own authority*. A second constitutional revolution had begun.

Parliament explained its rationale for the Militia Ordinance at greater length in a declaration of 6 June 1642. This stated that if the King refused to 'discharge [his] duty and trust', the two Houses were empowered 'to provide for the safety of the Parliament and peace of the kingdom'. It was Parliament's role not only 'to provide for the necessities, prevent the imminent dangers, and preserve the public peace and safety of the kingdom' but also 'to declare the King's pleasure in those things as are requisite thereunto'. The declaration then made a crucial distinction between the King's *person* and his *office*. It asserted that although the King, 'seduced by evil counsel', might 'in his own person oppose' the Houses, his 'supreme and royal pleasure' was nevertheless 'exercised and declared' in Parliament 'after a more eminent and obligatory manner than it can be by personal act or resolution of his own'. This distinction enabled Parliament to argue that their ordinances possessed the same legal force as statutes to which the King had assented. If need be, the Houses could govern alone.

These arguments marked a new and radical reinterpretation of medieval doctrines of the King's 'two bodies'. For the first time ever, they defined Parliament as the ultimate locus of sovereignty. The Militia Ordinance thus ushered in the second constitutional revolution of the 1640s, spanning the years 1642–7. This revolution was characterized by a claim that the two Houses of Parliament could if necessary exercise supreme power by themselves, *without the*

The confrontation between Charles's guards and London citizens, January 1642, was an important prelude to the Civil War.

King's consent. Between March 1642 and the end of the first Civil War, Parliament passed over 550 ordinances regulating such diverse matters as religious worship, military organization, local government, legal processes, financial levies and the press. Thus, if the 1530s had established the 'omnicompetence of statute', the period after March 1642 established the omnicompetence of ordinance. This inevitably had far-reaching effects on the nature and practice of government. At least in those parts of England which Parliament controlled, it brought radical changes in the existing administrative, financial and legal order. It is to these changes that we now turn.

V

Throughout the first Civil War, Charles continued to claim supreme civil and military authority. He raised troops by traditional means (the commissions of array) and carried his executive organs (the Privy Council, the Council of War, the legal and financial courts) with him, first to York and then to Oxford. Parliament, by contrast, had to build an executive machinery from scratch. It is necessary to examine in turn Parliament's central administration; its county administration; its financial system; and its management of the legal system.

In London, ultimate power and authority always remained with the two Houses of Parliament. But specific executive functions were delegated to a series of committees consisting mostly of representatives from both Houses. These central committees handled a vast range of business, but the most important can be divided into three categories: military; fiscal/punitive; and religious. The first of the military committees was the Committee of Safety, established on 4 July 1642 to advise Parliament's Lord General, the Earl of Essex, and to provide his army with cash and provisions. After Scotland entered the war on Parliament's side, this was replaced by the Committee of Both Kingdoms (later the Committee of Derby House) on 16 February 1644. The fiscal/punitive committees were designed both to raise money for Parliament's war effort and to punish its enemies. The earliest was the Committee for the Advance of Money (26 November 1642), which raised loans and imposed assessments from those who did not subscribe voluntarily. Much more draconian was the Sequestration Committee (27 March 1643), appointed to confiscate and administer the estates of 'delinquents' (Royalists and Catholics). But the yield from sequestrations proved relatively disappointing and the Committee for Compounding was therefore created in August 1645 to return lands to 'delinquents' on payment of a fine. Lastly, there were two committees whose main purpose was religious: the Committee for Scandalous Ministers which ejected Royalist clergy from their livings; and that for Plundered Ministers which provided support for 'godly' ministers expelled from Royalist areas. Thus, from 1642 Parliament developed a sophisticated and flexible executive apparatus based upon specialized committees.

Committees were also the linch-pin of Parliament's local administration. Apart from the two military committees, the above bodies all had exact counterparts in each county. In theory, these always remained answerable to the appropriate central committee, and ultimately to Parliament. In practice, however, they tended to be dominated by the 'county committees' established in each shire during the winter of 1642–3. Parliament originally intended these to provide troops and military supplies. But their powers grew to include raising taxes, enforcing religious reform, appointing JPs and sheriffs, and punishing Parliament's enemies. Never before had local governors wielded such extensive authority. The county committees became effectively omnipotent in those areas controlled by Parliament. But by the later 1640s they were almost universally loathed as an instrument of 'Roundhead tyranny'. To explain this, we must investigate Parliament's financial system, and its attitude to the law.

Parliament funded its military effort from two sources. First, the various punitive measures against 'delinquents' (especially sequestrations and compositions) had yielded a total of about £1·8 million by 1649. Second, Parliament introduced two direct taxes. An ordinance of 24 February 1643 ordered each county to pay a fixed weekly (later monthly) 'assessment', which the county committee then divided up between hundreds. This effectively became a land tax and closely resembled Ship Money. Far more novel was the 'new impost' (or 'excise') established on 22 July 1643. This taxed many consumables and the duties on such staple goods as meat, salt and beer were particularly detested. These two taxes imposed a crushing burden on the provinces: for example, by 1645–6 Kent paid more for each monthly assessment than in a whole year for Ship Money.

Even worse was Parliament's flouting of the rule of law in order to win the Civil War. Philip, Lord Wharton claimed in 1643 that the Parliamentarians 'were not tied to a law for these were times of necessity and imminent danger'. Both national and local committees were given powers outside the common law. They could search property and seize goods; they could billet soldiers arbitrarily; they could imprison those who resisted, without trial or cause shown. Parliamentarian troops and officials were granted an indemnity protecting them from all legal action against them. From May 1647 any attempt to obtain redress under the common law was simply overturned by a special Committee for Indemnity. No monarch had ever claimed such complete freedom from the law. Indeed, Parliament's pursuit of victory led it to break every clause in the Petition of Right. Small wonder, then, that by 1647–8 it was widely seen as far more tyrannical than Charles I had ever been. The Kentish petition of 11 May 1648 was typical in its plea that 'according to the fundamental constitution . . . we may . . . be governed . . . by the known and established laws of the kingdom and not otherwise'. These words precisely echoed Parliament's earlier complaints to the King. They reflected both a shattering realization that Parliamentarian rule was no better than Royalist, and a desperate yearning for peace. The various peace proposals advanced between 1642 and 1648, the nature of their terms and the reasons for their failure, must be considered.

VI

June 1642 saw King and Parliament adopt the basic constitutional positions which they were to defend throughout the first Civil War. The differences between them hinged on the extent to which the King's prerogatives and Parliament's privileges might be subjected to a 'mathematical' definition.

Parliament set out its terms in the *Nineteen Propositions* (1 June 1642). The key demands were contained in the first three propositions: that *all* Privy Councillors and 'great officers and ministers of state . . . may be approved of by both Houses of Parliament'; that 'the great affairs of the kingdom' be 'concluded or transacted' only by Parliament or by Privy Councillors chosen 'by approbation of both Houses of Parliament'; and that sixteen named officers of state be 'always . . . chosen' with Parliament's approval. Heading the list were the revived medieval offices of Lord High Steward and Lord High Constable which Parliament had probably earmarked for the Earls of Pembroke and Essex respectively. The remaining propositions included demands that all Privy Coun-

Table of Main Events

3 November 1640	Long Parliament assembles
15 February 1641	Triennial Act
11 May 1641	Act 'against the dissolving of Parliament without its own consent'
12 May 1641	Execution of Strafford
5 July 1641	Abolition of Courts of Star Chamber and High Commission
22 November 1641	Grand Remonstrance
5 March 1642	Militia Ordinance
1 June 1642	*Nineteen Propositions*
18 June 1642	Charles I's *Answer to the Nineteen Propositions*
1 February 1643	Oxford Propositions
24 November 1644	Uxbridge Propositions
13 July 1646	Newcastle Propositions
1 August 1647	*Heads of the Proposals*
14 December 1647	*Four Bills*
26 December 1647	King's 'Engagement' with the Scots
6 December 1648	Pride's Purge
4 January 1649	Parliament's 'Three Resolutions'
20 January 1649	Trial of Charles I opens
27 January 1649	Charles I sentenced to death
30 January 1649	Execution of Charles I
6 February 1649	Abolition of the House of Lords
7 February 1649	Abolition of the monarchy
13 February 1649	Council of State appointed
19 May 1649	England declared a 'Commonwealth'

cillors and judges swear to maintain the Petition of Right; that the King entrust the 'education' and 'marriage' of his children to Parliament; that he accept the Militia Ordinance; that no new peer attend the Lords without Parliament's consent; and that there be such 'a reformation . . . of the Church government and liturgy as both Houses of Parliament shall advise'. Faced with a King whom it no longer trusted, Parliament sought to circumscribe royal powers and to devise a watertight formula for limited, constitutional monarchy.

Charles's *Answer to the Nineteen Propositions* (18 June 1642) was a truly classic defence of the 'ancient constitution'. The English polity, he declared, blended 'absolute monarchy, aristocracy and democracy' to provide 'the conveniences of all three without the inconveniences of any one'. It was therefore essential that the 'three estates' of King, Lords and Commons 'run jointly on in their proper channel'. According to the kingdom's fundamental laws, 'government . . . [was] [en]trusted to the King'. He had 'power of treaties of war and peace, of making peers, of choosing officers of state, judges for law, commanders for forts and castles, giving commissions for raising men, to make war abroad, or to prevent . . . invasions'. Charles insisted that the *Nineteen Propositions* formed a 'ladder by which our just, ancient, regal power is . . . to be fetched down to the ground'. They would thus subvert 'the fundamental laws and . . . excellent constitution of this kingdom'. It was Parliament, not the King, who sought to innovate and to overthrow the natural balance of the constitution.

Although Parliament's subsequent demands became both wider and more specific, its basic position did not change. Thus, the Oxford Propositions (1 February 1643) required in addition the disbandment of Royalist forces, further religious reforms (including the abolition of episcopacy), the dismissal of certain named Privy Councillors, and several specific appointments to the judiciary. The Uxbridge Propositions (24 November 1644) added the demand that Charles sign the *Solemn League and Covenant* (sanctioning religious changes 'according to the Word of God and the example of the best reformed churches'), extended the list of culpable royal advisers, and exempted named 'malignants' from pardon. Growing fear of Essex's ambition also prompted the deletion of the Steward and the Constable from the 'great officers of state' to be approved by Parliament. Finally, after the King's surrender, the Newcastle Propositions (13 July 1646) explicitly sought to limit the King's legislative veto. They also demanded the establishment of a Presbyterian Church for three years and Parliamentary control over the militia and over state appointments for twenty years. It was assumed that this would cover the rest of Charles's natural life – further evidence that Parliament wished to restrain him *personally* rather than his *office*.

But always the King's answer was the same: he would not abandon episcopacy entirely, and he adamantly refused to sacrifice his command of the armed forces, his choice of ministers and his veto over legislation. Such powers were, he claimed, 'inseparably and undoubtedly inherent to the Crown by the laws of this nation'. Time and again, negotiations were deadlocked over these issues. Finally, in the summer of 1647, the army – in conjunction with a radical faction in Parliament – decided to offer Charles fresh terms, which were known as the *Heads of the Proposals*.

The coalition which promoted the *Heads* was led in the Lords by Viscount Saye and Sele and Lord Wharton, and in the Commons and the Army Council by Cromwell and Ireton. By mid-1647 these men felt that Parliament's existing leaders had betrayed the army and the 'cause' for which it had fought. In a bid to gain ascendancy, they therefore devised an alternative programme which would both enshrine their own ideals and, they hoped, win the King's consent. The *Heads* challenged two principles which had underpinned all Parliament's earlier proposals. The first was an assumption that the two Houses formed the natural check on the King's powers. In the search for a 'mathematical security', it was Parliament which devised the mathematics and which would guarantee the security. Executive authority was to be transferred *from* the King *to* the two Houses. The *Heads* rejected this maxim. While granting Parliament control over officers of state and over the militia for ten years, they clearly foresaw the danger of a Parliamentarian tyranny and therefore envisaged biennial Parliaments sitting for no more than 240 days. Second, Parliament had hitherto demanded religious reforms leading towards a Presbyterian Church. The *Heads*, by contrast, sought toleration of Independent congregations outside the Presbyterian structure, and even permitted episcopacy provided it lacked coercive powers. The *Heads* thus

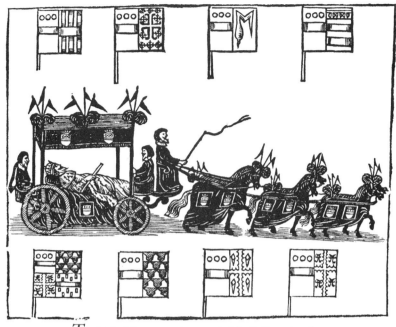

The Earl of Essex, captain-general of the Parliamentary forces, 1642-5, buried with quasi-monarchical honours, 1646.

expressed a quite different vision of the future from that embodied in Parliament's earlier terms. Their appeal to the King was further enhanced by clauses which exempted only seven named Royalists from pardon (compared with 58 under the Newcastle Propositions), and preserved the royal veto over legislation. Of all the terms offered Charles during the 1640s, the *Heads* sought the least Parliamentary constraint on royal powers.

But, once again, Charles's refusal to surrender control over ministerial appointments and over the militia made him reject even these attractive propositions. Shortly afterwards, and for the same reason, he rejected Parliament's minimum terms contained in the *Four Bills* (14 December 1647). These would, he insisted, 'divest him of all sovereignty'. Instead he signed an 'Engagement' with the Scots which left his civil and military powers intact. Charles confirmed the *Solemn League and Covenant* and agreed to introduce Presbyterianism in England for three years. The Scots in return promised military assistance against the English Parliament.

This Scottish invasion fused with a 'revolt of the provinces' against Parliamentarian tyranny to produce the second Civil War of 1648. Yet, even when Parliamentary armies had emerged victorious, the vast majority of MPs could still not contemplate a settlement without the King. They saw no alternative but to resume negotiations with him, and so in September 1648 they offered Charles terms more lenient than the Newcastle Propositions. This time, Charles agreed to introduce Presbyterianism for three years and to surrender control of the militia for twenty. Despite hints that the King might revoke these concessions, most

MPs wanted to continue negotiations. This was the closest they had yet come to a 'mathematical security'. They wanted to forget the Civil Wars and to reach a settlement. But there was a minority, concentrated in the army, which felt very differently.

VII

This brings us to the constitutional revolution of 1648–9: the purging of Parliament, the trial and execution of Charles I, and the abolition of monarchy and the House of Lords. This third constitutional revolution altered English government far more profoundly than the previous two. Instead of trying to define the relationship between Crown and Parliament – first with and then without Charles's consent – the King was now removed entirely and a republican regime established. Why, if Parliament had taken up arms in 1642 explicitly to *defend* the office of King, did the Civil War lead to a series of such dramatic changes?

To answer this question, we must examine the growing political involvement of the army. That process began in the spring and summer of 1647 when Parliament's attempts to disband troops without pay led the army to demand the impeachment of eleven MPs, to threaten a purge of the Commons, and to begin talks with the King. But Charles's rejection of the *Heads of the Proposals* and his 'Engagement' with the Scots (see above) confirmed his incorrigible duplicity. Throughout the first Civil War, Charles had sought to divide his enemies by negotiating with all sides simultaneously. If necessary, he was quite prepared to accept aid from 'papists'. In September 1643 he signed a 'Cessation' with the Irish rebels. His letters to his Queen, Henrietta Maria, captured at Naseby and later published by Parliament as *The King's Cabinet Opened*, revealed his secret dealings with the Irish, the French and even the Pope. Charles's subsequent attempt to reverse the outcome of the first Civil War by waging a second convinced army leaders that further talks would be not merely futile but *evil*. At a great prayer meeting at Windsor Castle in April 1648 the officers condemned their earlier 'cursed carnal conferences . . . with the King' and resolved 'to call Charles Stuart, that man of blood, to an account for that blood he had shed'. The King's defeat in the second Civil War proved that he was, in Cromwell's words, 'a man against whom the Lord hath witnessed'. It was now the army's duty, as God's instrument, to bring Charles to justice.

These doctrines of the King's 'blood-guilt' were derived from Old Testament texts such as Numbers, XXXV, 33: 'Blood it defileth the land: and the land cannot be cleansed of the blood that is shed therein, but by the blood of him that shed it'. Such ideas unleashed savage, elemental forces. Never before had they directly influenced English political developments. But in 1648–9 they were used to justify fundamental constitutional change. Even in the late 1640s, most people still felt an instinctive reverence towards the monarch as 'God's anointed'. Early modern England was remarkable for its 'momentum of obedience', its ingrained belief that 'the powers that be are ordained of God'. The *only* force which could cut through such a belief was another, deeper, religious imperative – the need to expiate the King's 'blood-guilt'. By the autumn of 1648, this imperative had convinced many army leaders that the only acceptable 'mathematical security' was Charles's death.

Comparative Chart of the Main Peace Terms

	Nineteen Propositions	Oxford Propositions	Uxbridge Propositions	Newcastle Propositions	Heads of the Proposals	Four Bills
Parliaments	Triennial Act stands	Triennial Act stands	Triennial Act stands	Triennial Act stands	Triennial Act repealed; biennial Parliaments	Triennial Act stands
Privy Councillors	Parliament to approve	—	—	—		—
Officers of State	Parliament to approve 16	—	Parliament to nominate 13	Parliament to nominate 13	Parliament to nominate for 10 years	
Militia	King to accept Militia Ordinance	King to settle with Parliament's advice	To be settled by commissioners named by Parliament	Parliament to control for 20 years	Parliament to control for 10 years	Parliament to control for 20 years
Church government	Reformed with Parliament's advice	Bishops etc. abolished	Bishops etc. abolished; reforms advised by Westminster Assembly	Bishops etc. abolished; Presbyterian church for 3 yrs	Bishops etc. cannot coerce no Presbyterian church	Bishops etc. abolished; Presbyterian church for 3 yrs
Papists	Existing laws to be enforced	Existing laws to be enforced	Existing laws to be enforced	Existing laws to be enforced	Existing laws to be abolished & new ones made	Existing laws to be enforced
Royalists not to be pardoned	—	2	58	58	7	58
Dismissals from office	—	2 for life	48 for life	48 for life	Parliament's enemies for 5 years	48 for life

When, therefore, the House of Commons voted to continue negotiations with him, the army carried out the purge which it had threatened in 1647. On 6 December 1648, in a violation of Parliamentary privilege far more drastic than the King's attempt on the five members, Colonel Thomas Pride arrested 45 MPs and secluded 186, while a further 86 withdrew in protest. In late December the 'Rump' of the Commons passed an ordinance creating a court to try the King. When this was defeated in the Lords, the Rump passed three resolutions (4 January 1649) which totally redefined the institutions of English government. It was resolved that 'all just power' derived from 'the people'; that the Commons possessed 'supreme power'; and that 'whatever' it enacted had 'the force of law' even without the consent of King or Lords. Two days later, the Rump used this authority to establish a High Court of Justice. When the trial opened on 20 January, Charles was charged with harbouring 'a wicked design to erect and uphold in himself an unlimited and tyrannical power to rule according to his will and to overthrow the rights and liberties of the people', and with 'traitorously and maliciously [levying] war against Parliament, and the people therein represented'. He was therefore to be impeached as 'a tyrant, traitor and murderer, and a public and implacable enemy to the Commonwealth of England'.

When he heard the last phrase, Charles 'laughed . . . in the face of the Court'. He maintained this sovereign contempt throughout the eight-day trial. He insisted that the Court had no authority to try him: it contravened both God's law ('for . . . obedience unto Kings is . . . strictly commanded in both

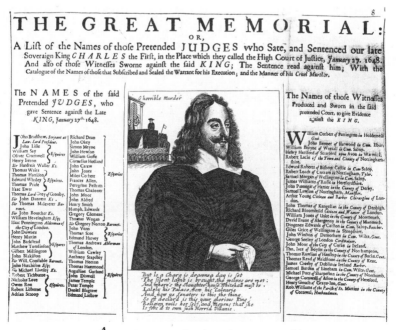

A Royalist report, identifying the men responsible
for the regicide.

Olever Crumwells Cabinet Councell Discoverd

A	The:Divell	G	Cor: Holland *ho other*
B	Olever:Cromwell	H	I:Iones *ho other of him*
C	Io: Bradshaw Pres:	I	Lisle
D	Tho: Scott *no other of him*	K	Say
E	Coll: Harrison	L	Hugh Petters
F	Coll: Barksted *ho other*	M	I:Goodwin

1649.

*Royalist propaganda has some unlikely members of Cromwell's
Cabinet Council of 1649.*

the Old and New Testament') and the common law (which affirmed that 'the King could do no wrong'). Far from expressing the will of the people, the Court had 'never asked . . . the tenth man in the kingdom'. It thus threatened 'the true liberty' of the subject, which consisted 'not in the power of government, but in living under . . . such a government as may give themselves the best assurance of their lives, and property of their goods'. Charles pledged himself 'to defend the fundamental laws of [the] kingdom', and argued that if the army might arbitrarily try the King, then no 'free-born subject of England' could 'call life or anything he possesseth his own'. By identifying his own fate so closely with 'the welfare and liberty of [his] people' Charles scored a massive propaganda victory and immeasurably strengthened the long-term appeal of Royalism.

But in the short term nothing could save him. The High Court ignored and ultimately silenced Charles's protests. On 27 January it sentenced him to death. Only 59 'regicides' signed the King's death warrant, and they implemented the will of but a tiny minority. Charles skilfully exploited this fact in his final speech on the scaffold. He defended the 'liberty and freedom' of the people, condemned 'the power of the sword', and swore to 'die a Christian according to the profession of the Church of England'. Then, in a masterly peroration, Charles portrayed himself as 'the martyr of the people'. His cultivation of a 'popular' image proved highly successful. The deep reverence which the vast majority still felt for monarchy was hauntingly expressed in the eerie groan let out by onlookers as the axe fell. Thereafter, the posthumous (and probably ghosted) collection of Charles's speeches and meditations, the *Eikon Basilike*, soon ran into many editions. Charles thus served the cause of English monarchy far more effectively in death than in life, and his final vision of a constitutional monarch guarding popular liberties and the Church of England provided the basis for the Restoration Settlement.

In 1649, however, the initiative lay with the Rump, supported by the army. Immediately after the regicide, the Rump began to amputate now redundant constitutional limbs. The destruction of the monarchy and the House of Lords followed naturally from the three resolutions of 4 January which had deprived both of their legislative role. Equally, there was still a danger that Royalists might use these institutions to destabilize the new regime. The Rump therefore resolved that the Lords and the office of King were both 'useless' and 'dangerous', and abolished them on 6 and 7 February respectively. A Council of State was appointed on 13 February for one year, to perform the executive functions of the Crown. Finally, on 19 May, England was declared 'a Commonwealth and Free State . . . without any King or House of Lords'. The nation which in 1640 had been governed by a blend of 'personal' and 'mixed' monarchy was now, for the first and last time in its history, a republic.

VIII

The 1640s thus had an immediate and profound impact on the nature of English government. But how many of these radical changes endured? The constitutional revolution of 1648–9 rapidly proved disastrous, for it robbed English government of the legitimacy which the King alone could provide. The Interregnum (1649–60) graphically showed that a republican regime was unable to generate stability. England had four separate constitutions during these years, and finally descended into complete chaos in 1659–60. By the spring of 1660 a restoration of the monarchy seemed the only alternative to anarchy. A free, bi-cameral Parliament (the Convention) was elected in April. On 8 May, in a bid to restore stable, legitimate government, this Parliament declared Charles II to have been King from the moment of his father's death. Officially, the Interregnum had not existed.

The Restoration Settlement overturned the constitutional revolutions of 1642–7 and 1648–9 but left that of 1640–1 intact. Charles II accepted all those reforms to which his father had assented: a (weakened) Triennial Act remained in force; the prerogative Courts of Star Chamber and High Commission were not re-established; the Privy Council never regained its judicial authority; and Charles agreed not to levy prerogative taxes. Yet royal discretionary powers still remained considerable after 1660. These years also witnessed a remarkable revitalization of traditional institutions of government, at both central and local levels. Parliament's ubiquitous committees were destroyed forever. Once more, England's executive consisted of the King and Privy Council, its legislature of the King-in-Parliament. In the provinces, power was again wielded by Lords Lieutenant and their deputies, and especially by Justices of the Peace. Familiar legal courts, such as assizes and quarter sessions, regained all their old vibrancy.

But the period after 1660 saw more than a straightforward return to the situation of 1641. The destruction of the prerogative courts and the discrediting of Parliament as a desirable check on the Crown enabled local government to gain an unprecedented autonomy from the centre. Responsibility for many administrative tasks – including the collection of taxes, regulation of the militia, enforcement of ecclesiastical, social and economic legislation, and control of the movement of labour – was now entrusted to provincial magistrates whose decisions could not be challenged in the central courts. This devolution was a direct consequence of local resentment against the incursions of *both* sides during the Civil War (see above).

Yet in one sense, the Restoration Settlement was almost too successful. It restored the 'ancient constitution', but restored with it all the fudges and ambiguities which had led to Civil War. In particular, the English polity still lacked safeguards against an inept or deranged monarch. The locus of sovereignty remained uncertain, and the fundamental problem of what to do if the monarch tried to subvert the constitution was left unresolved. The Civil War and Interregnum had shown that a search for 'mathematical security' could run hideously out of control. During Charles II's reign this search was tacitly abandoned in the hope that painful definitions might be avoided. But under James II the tensions inherent within the English constitution precipitated another revolution. Faced with a stark choice between its King and its Church, the majority of the English élite chose the latter. In the wake of the 'Glorious Revolution', a body of legislation culminating in the Act of Settlement (1701) limited and defined royal powers. These measures – which compelled the King to be an Anglican, to spend Parliamentary subsidies as Parliament wished, not to manipulate the judiciary, and not to pardon those whom the Commons impeached – marked a decisive shift away from 'personal monarchy' towards a fully 'mixed monarchy'. England had at last achieved a 'mathematical security' against the vagaries of its monarchs.

CHAPTER III

The Impact of Puritanism

JOHN MORRILL

Between 1640 and 1649 some unthinkable things happened. The King was put on trial and publicly beheaded. The House of Lords was abolished. And many of the distinguishing marks of organized religion in England and Wales were uprooted. The Church of England, which had emerged from the Reformation a century before, and had evolved in important ways over a thousand years, was dismantled. The Archbishop of Canterbury preceded his Supreme Governor to the block. Many other bishops were imprisoned or exiled. Episcopacy itself was abolished, and the lands and possessions of the bishoprics and of the cathedral churches were sold off, mainly to property speculators in London. Ordinances were passed making it a criminal offence to use the Book of Common Prayer, or for Christians to gather together to celebrate in song and prayer the anniversaries of the birth, death and Resurrection of their Saviour. The interiors of parish churches were ripped out, completing a process begun at the Reformation and transforming them into whitewashed auditoria. Almost a third of the parish clergy were ejected from their livings. The great majority of those

*T*he Protestation Oath was one of many attempts to make clear the threat of 'popery' to the integrity of English Protestantism.

The Souldiers in their passage to York turn unto reformers pull down Popish pictures, break down rayles, turn altars into Tables

Any signs of 'popish idolatry' found in parish churches were ruthlessly destroyed by the army.

who went to church at all, still went to a parish church, but an increasing number opted out; they joined voluntary congregations of like-thinkers in private houses and barns, or went out on to hillsides and moors to listen to itinerant preachers. Although the *right* of individuals to opt out of the state Church, and the *right* of liberty of conscience and public witness were not yet formally established, they had become a reality, backed by an Army leadership that had the muscle and the determination to make it happen.

In 1640, no one foresaw, or could have foreseen, the regicide, or the abolition of the monarchy or the House of Lords. But a minority could and did foresee quite a lot of these religious changes. The abolition of episcopacy and Prayer Book, the 'cleansing' of the churches of popish remnants and of unworthy ministers, were seen as necessary first stages in a process that would transform England into a showcase of godly living, and, quite possibly, mark a crucial stage in the working out of God's plan to send His Son back to reign in person for a thousand years before the final ending of the world at the Day of Judgement. It was this visionary side to Puritanism in 1640 which constituted the real fire in the belly of those who were prepared not only to enumerate Charles's failings in all his doings as King, not only to use Parliamentary leverage to demand that he be made more strictly accountable at law and required to hearken to reliable counsellors, but also to use force of arms to make it happen. There was virtually no one in Parliament in 1641 or 1642 who envisaged the granting of religious liberty to those who dissented from the teaching or practice of the Established Church; but there were many who sought, alongside a restabilized and rebalanced civil polity, a reconstituted and re-formed Church. The strength of language from MPs and preachers to the

Parliament is testimony enough: 'religion is our *primum quaerite*, for all things else are but etceteras to it', said one MP; 'we have spent our time only in pulling off the bark, and snatching the boughs and branches of popery, and that will do no good, for they will grow thicker and harder; the only way is to fall to our work in earnest, and lay the axe to the root', said another; 'look thoroughly at what is amiss and pluck up every plant that God hath not planted', warned a preacher, listing prelacy and the Prayer Book amongst the indigenous weeds. So great was the press of petitions from hundreds of parishes across the country complaining about innovations and about the intrusive and bullying tactics used by Laudian bishops and their henchmen that the Bishop of Lincoln (a longstanding bitter personal enemy of Laud) wrote to a group of Cambridge dons and preachers associated with powerful peerage families asking them to advise his Upper House Committee in their 'examination of all innovations in doctrine or discipline introduced into the Church without law since the Reformation and if their lordships shall find it behoveful for the good of the Church and state *to examine after the degrees and perfection of the Reformation itself.*' Episcopacy, the Church courts, the Prayer Book were all open to criticism. The Grand Remonstrance itself saw no need to investigate failings of secular governance before the accession of Charles I, and no one found it necessary to examine the perfection of the ancient constitution. Yet the Laudians had so undermined confidence in the Established Church that the restoration of *its* ancient constitution was not enough for those who made war on the King.

The militancy of religious reformers in the early 1640s has disconcerted many historians. Reluctant to see Laud as other than the efficient champion of a school of thought within Anglicanism that had evolved naturally from its inception, and perhaps as the heir to humanist impulses within the English Reformation process, these historians have been tempted to write off the Puritan drive of the 1640s as the opportunism of the few, and as an orchestrated campaign by those whose main objective was the removal of the bishops as a loyalist bloc-vote in the House of Lords. But this is to misunderstand Laudianism and its impact. It understates both the hostility of the defenders of the *via media*, established by the Elizabethan settlement, to the innovations of recent years; and it underestimates the strength and spontaneity of provincial Puritan activity – in petitioning and in orchestrated acts of iconoclasm. Thus even those who were to fight and die for Church as well as King in the 1640s dissociated themselves from recent 'innovation' and fought for what Charles I, in abandoning Laud to imprisonment and execution, called 'the true reformed Protestant religion by law established, without any connivance of popery or innovation'. Those who spoke in Parliament, or who, in a majority of English counties, organized petitions to King or Parliament in defence of episcopacy or the Book of Common Prayer, were careful to dissociate themselves from what one of them (Lord Falkland) called the 'English popery' of Laud and his colleagues.

By 'English popery' they meant first and foremost Laudian attempts to reclaim for churchmen much of the wealth and power taken from the Church at the Reformation, and their attempts to assert clerical authority over the laity; together with a ceremonialism that insisted upon general observance of forms of worship that many felt were incompatible with divine injunction, and which certainly changed the developed practice of most parishes. A majority of the peers and a strong minority of the Commons never abandoned an ecclesiastical ancient constitutionalism and Prayer Book sentimentalism. But many others were too shaken by what had happened to accept that the Church would ever be made safe for Protestantism unless prelacy (lordly/Laudly power in the bishops) and liturgical compromise were overthrown.

A minority of committed reformers were convinced that Christ's Second Coming was imminent (for example, one preacher published in 1642 a sermon entitled *The Personal Reign of Christ upon the Earth*, predicting the imminent and immanent personal monarchy of Jesus). Many more preachers harangued MPs at their monthly Fast Days on the parallels between the way God intervened in the history of the Jewish people, as narrated in the Old Testament, and modern times. It was God's way to use prophets to indicate His will to the Israelites but to leave them free to obey (and be rewarded) or to disobey (and be punished, as by slavery in Egypt or captivity in Babylon). In the same way, it was asserted that God was now making clear that the people of England were being invited to complete the Reformation, to turn England into a commonwealth in which the Church was free to preach the gospel and the state equipped to command obedience to that gospel. If the English nation turned from past compromises and errors to obedience to this command, God would reward them with peace and prosperity; otherwise they could expect to be delivered over to antichristian terrors. As Robert Baillie put it in his tract *The Canterburians Self-Conviction* (1641), they would see the Bible replaced by the Mass, Magna Carta by the laws of Castile, and the nobility and gentry would find themselves in the chain-gangs of Peru and the galleys of the Mediterranean. It is important for us to grasp that many MPs took such warnings literally. They did not see themselves as making armchair choices between alternative forms of worship and Church government as we might between different television channels. They were making ultimate choices between Good and Evil, between Eternal Life and Eternal Damnation.

At a less demanding level, many MPs who initially favoured the curtailment of episcopal power and the purging of the Prayer Book of its residual popish dross, were moved to support a more complete reformation by Scottish pressure. Gratitude to the Scots for bringing an end to the Personal Rule, and some sympathy for the view that a greater uniformity of religion in all three kingdoms would make for greater long-term stability in their relations, brought some to support the proposals inspired by the Scots for a reform of the Church 'root and branch' in 1641. This fatally weakened the prospect of compromise amongst English Puritans around schemes for 'primitive' episcopacy in the course of 1641.

These schemes took two forms. One favoured by many future Royalists would have left the old order (and many of the same men) in place, but would have stripped the episcopal office of most of its autocratic powers and turned the bishops into salaried chairmen of diocesan Boards of Governors. A majority of the future Parliamentarian MPs and many leading preachers (including Stephen Marshall, Edmund Calamy and Cornelius Burges) favoured a scheme by which the whole existing order was abolished and a new one set up. Dioceses would be replaced by county jurisdictions run by representative clergy presided over by a minister known as the superintendent or (since the term was used in the New Testament) *episcopos* or bishop, whose powers of independent action would be heavily circumscribed. Hope that all the godly would coalesce around this scheme was evaporating month by month, however, as the country veered into war, and in 1642 the King's opponents committed themselves to no more than the abolition of the old order and the calling of a national synod to determine what to put in its place.

Thus, at least in regard to Church government, the Puritans of 1640–2 knew what they would not have, but not what they would have. The impulse to uproot superstition, idolatry, popery was overwhelming. It meant ripping out altar rails, taking hammers to stone statues, carved roof bosses and images in glass. It meant ensuring sound preaching twice every Sunday in every church. It meant restricting access to holy communion to those whose outward lives displayed an inner Faith. It meant the suspension and eventual repeal of the existing form of Church government. But there never was a moment when even all those committed to godly reformation came close to agreeing on an alternative form of Church government.

Behind the fumbling efforts to establish a primitive episcopacy lay two divergent ecclesiologies. One aspired to a Scottish model, derived from the Presbyterian system developed at Calvin's Geneva; the other looked to those who had lived in, experienced, or simply admired at a distance, the achievements of the Congregationalist or Independent Churches in New England or the Netherlands. The two had much in common, and as the 1640s unfolded, they agreed upon a manual for worship, a catechism (or summary of belief), and a Confession of Faith that almost all of them could use. All these documents were developed, agreed and promulgated by the Westminster Assembly in the mid-1640s. Most could agree too on some aspects of Church government: the need for elders to run the parish alongside the minister; the essential parity of all those in the ministry; the absolute centrality of Bible-reading and exposition of the word of God through preaching; the nature of the moral law and the meaning of the Commandments of the Old and New Testament. But on one fundamental point no agreement was ever possible: did ultimate authority in the Visible Church (in the choosing of ministers, admission to the sacraments of baptism and holy communion, Church membership and excommunication) lie in each group of self-consciously godly Christians gathered within a structure of autonomous parishes, or did it lie in regional and national assemblies of the Church? This was the reef that shipwrecked the hopes of Puritan unity by and after 1645. In 1641–2 all that lay in the future.

It is implicit in what has been said so far that the real issue in the early 1640s was about what sort of state Church would emerge from the recriminations following the collapse of the Laudian Church. There was no campaign within Parliament, and very little outside it, for religious liberty, for toleration of those who did not want to be part of the state Church. There was a rapid growth in the number of Baptist Churches (assemblies of those who believed that membership of any congregation should be a voluntary act of submission by someone sufficiently adult to be able to make a clear personal commitment, potently represented by submission to the rite of adult baptism or incorporation). But membership of all such assemblies had probably barely topped 1,000 at the time war broke out. The English Civil War began as a struggle between two movements committed to two different visions of the confessional state, two

The years 1641-2 saw a nationwide attack on Roman Catholics and the destruction of their chapels and 'superstitious books and pictures'.

visions of how all men and women should be compelled to be members of a national Church which would seek to bring them to a loving obedience to the will of God as vouchsafed by rival interpretations of scripture and the Christian tradition.

On the one side stood the Anglican-Royalists. They were committed to the ancient constitution of the Church of England, its established liturgy, its encouragement of all to gather at the Lord's table, its appropriation of regional and local cultures to give meaning and value to the daily and recreational lives of the people as a whole. On the other side stood Puritan-Parliamentarians. They were committed to completing the process of Reformation, bringing to the Church in England the cleansing, scouring power of scriptural literalness. They wished to bring to bear the austere Protestant experience of Scotland or of the howling wilderness of New England. They sought to separate those with an assurance of salvation who might gather round the Holy Table, from the reprobate majority who were to sit behind, pondering the injunctions to obedience, which, be they saved or damned, was still God's will for them, and bringing to bear in the lives of all men and women the need to choose between the profaneness and sinfulness of traditional pastimes and recreations and the order and decency of the lives of the godly.

Throughout the 1640s, the Puritans kept up the unrelenting pressure on the old Church. A bill for the abolition of episcopacy was moved in Parliament in late 1642 and a demand that the King agree to such a bill was included in the terms offered to him at Oxford early in 1643: this remained part of the formal negotiating stance of the two Houses until the summer of 1647 and, for the majority of MPs, even after that. Most of the bishops had fled, and

The 2 of May. 1643. y⁰ Croſſe in Cheapeſide was pulled downe, a Troope of Horſe & 2 Companies of foote wayted to garde it & at y⁰ fall of y⁰ tope Croſſe dromes beat tru-pets blew & multitudes of Capes warre throwne in y⁰ Ayre, & a greate Shoute of People with ioy, y⁰ 2 of May the Almana- ke ſareth, was y⁰ invention of the Croſſe, & 6 day at night was the Leaden Popes burnt, in the pla- -ce where it ſtood with ringinge e⁰ Bells, & a greate Acclamation & no hurt done in all these actions.

*T*he Civil War saw the completion of the process of stripping the churches and public places of all 'monuments of idolatry and superstition', as here at Cheapside in London.

none operated from his cathedral city outside Royalist territory after 1642. Archbishop Laud languished in the Tower until the summer of 1644 when he was tried by impeachment before the House of Lords, only to defend himself so brilliantly (like Strafford earlier) that his enemies were forced to switch to an attainder (a simple legislative act taking away his life without due process of law). In January 1645, like Strafford before him (May 1641) and the King after him (January 1649), Laud was publicly beheaded. He was the only bishop to be executed, although others (most notably Matthew Wren of Ely who was to remain in the Tower until 1660) endured long periods in prison. The bishops' land was all sold (and shortly after so too was the land of the cathedral chapters). Many of the cathedrals were commandeered as barracks, prisons or warehouses. By 1649 some 2,300 ministers had been removed from their livings by Parliamentary committees on charges of Laudian activities in the 1630s, failure to accept the religious values of the 1640s, preaching for the royal interest, or for gross moral turpitude. The proceedings resulting in these deprivations were often exceptionally arbitrary, and indeed it has been suggested that the fact that the highest proportion of deprived ministers came from London or the Puritan heartlands of East Anglia, tells us a lot more about the composition of local committees than it does about the distribution of theologically unsound or of drunken and depraved clergy. Wherever vacancies were created, there was a likelihood that the Parliamentary Committee for Plundered Ministers would impose its own man (set up to find livings for Puritans ejected in Royalist areas, it became a body that interfered on behalf of godly ministers in general).

From the mid-1640s, it was a criminal offence for anyone to use the Book of Common Prayer, to celebrate the old round of Christian festivals (Christmas, Easter, Whit etc.), and many prosecutions followed across the country. In 1641, many individuals in parishes up and down the country took the law into their own hands and ripped out altar rails and other trappings of Laud's 'beauty of holiness'. In 1643–6 a second round of iconoclasm took place, this time supervised by itinerant commissioners briefed to remove all 'monuments and images of idolatry and superstition'. Men like William Dowsing, appointed commissioner for East Anglia, visited two or three parishes a day, personally supervised or left instruction for the removal of stained glass windows, of stone and wood carvings of angels and saints (even on roof bosses), defaced Norman fonts and chiselled from medieval tombs phrases such as *orate pro anima mea* (pleas to the living to remember the dead in their prayers). In some churches – such as Clare in Suffolk – Dowsing destroyed more than 1,000 images; there was not one amongst the 250 churches he recorded visiting, which he left untouched.

Everything that could be done by ordinance and executive action was done. Yet by 1649 Puritanism was in disarray. The prospects of turning the nation from the things of the flesh to the things of the spirit, of teaching all men their duties to God and compelling them to an obedience to those duties seemed to most as unrealizable as ever. The problems for the victorious Parliamentarians took three forms: the resilience of Anglicanism; internal divisions within Calvinist-Puritanism; and the spread of heresy and separatism.

Those who set out to replace the Established Church and its forms with something more austerely Protestant found the resilience of 'folk Anglicanism' baffling and frustrating. The panzer divisions of English Puritanism came up against some wily guerrillas enjoying widespread popular support. Far from being treated as patriots and liberators, the Puritan hot-gospellers were confronted by widespread non-co-operation and foot-dragging. In many parishes, the ministers were persuaded to continue to use the Book of Common Prayer especially for the rites of passage (baptism, marriage and burial) and for quarterly holy communions; and the prohibition on the celebration of Christmas and Easter was also widely flouted (many churchwardens' accounts continuing to record money spent on bays and holly and other decoration for festival days.) There was no great campaign for the preservation of episcopacy in the later 1640s (though many men intending to serve as ministers still chose to seek out retired bishops to ordain them before they sought out Presbyterian orders); but there is evidence of massive support for the old liturgies and old practices. This has been termed 'folk Anglicanism', but it might just as well be called congregational (or even Independent!) Anglicanism, stemming from deep resentments at outside interference in the life of the parish.

While godly minorities might welcome the assistance of county committees in imposing their wills, the interventions were frequently counter-productive. The records of the Cheshire committees, for example, find them complaining that they could only maintain their nominees in their parsonages by stationing permanent garrisons in the parishes, admitting that imposed ministers were regularly being denied tithes and that the commissioners did not have the resources to deal with so widespread an abuse; and their attempts to secure a living for one of the most respected Cheshire Puritans, Dr John Ley, a veteran

*The King defends the trunk of the tree of true religion, but the
puritans pick at the roots and hew off the branches.*

of the Westminster Assembly, was no nearer attainment in the summer of 1649
than it had been when they first ordered it three years earlier, despite a stream
of orders from central committees in London. The parish had protected the
man installed by the convicted Royalist gentleman who owned the right of
presentation.

Much of this may be less deep traditional piety than a demonstration
of dissent from the actions of the deeply unpopular Parliamentary regimes

of the later 1640s and a yearning for the good old days. Nor should the new-style services developed in the Directory of Worship published in 1645, with its emphasis not on the antiphonal praying and chanting of set prayers and psalms by minister and congregation, but on the lengthy sermonizing and extempore praying of the minister on the biblical texts he had chosen, be seen as anything but counter-productive: in the 1640s, all too literally, the Puritans may have been preaching only to the converted. But the extent to which this third and fourth generation to grow up under the 1559 religious settlement, had a genuine affection for Prayer-book Anglicanism accommodated to particular local conditions, should not be underestimated.

The experiences of many Puritan ministers in the 1640s bears out this gloomy sense of evangelical optimism turning to a widespread sense of futility and failure by the end of the decade. Petitions like this one from the minister of Stretham in the heartland of Puritanism, just three miles from Cromwell's Ely, exist for every county and reveal the bitter antipathies that were building up. It is dated January 1647 and was addressed to Parliament:

> That, in pursuance of the Directory [of Worship] and the National Covenant, your petitioner acquainted his People, the Lord's Day before, that they should not observe Christmas Day, because a penalty is laid on those ministers who do not observe the Directory, and by it Holy Days are not to be continued. Yet many of them, on Christmas Day last, brought in Mr John Cole, a soldier, to preach to them; and in the afternoon . . . they brought him in to preach again . . . or make your petitioner preach, which he did for quietness sake. And again on the next day, contrary to the Directory which your petitioner had read unto them, and his entreaty of them, they sung a dead corpse at the Church gate; whereupon your petitioner turning aside from them into a neighbour's house, they fetched him out thence by force, brought him to the grave, abused him speaking to them, threatened to bury him alive . . . to the endangering of his life, the affronting him in his ministry, obstruction of reformation, contempt of ordinance and the dishonour of Parliament.

If things were going that badly in Cambridgeshire, it is easy to imagine the problems of a godly minister imposed from without on a parish in a strongly royalist area, with an embittered convicted Royalist squire in the adjacent manor house, as he tried to separate the sheep around the communion table from the goatish majority who scowled or stayed away.

What further corroded the morale of the godly, as well as greatly weakening their evangelism in practical ways, was the internal disputes which arose from the debates on Church government at the Westminster Assembly in the mid-1640s. We have already seen that that assembly was highly successful in agreeing on a form of worship, on catechisms, confessions of faith and other formularies. But when they attempted to determine, from a close study of scripture, the prescriptions Christ had laid down for the government of his Church, they reached an impasse. The non-negotiable issue became the right of each parish to self-determination in choosing ministers and in disciplining its errant members. The inherent tensions over this issue broke out into open and increasingly bitter dispute with the publication by five members of the Assembly (all men who had spent the 1630s in exile in the Netherlands and who all enjoyed the support of

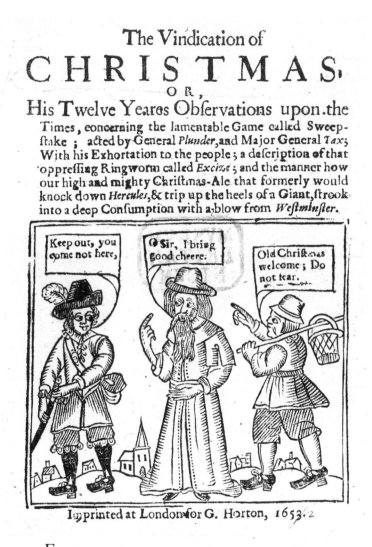

The Vindication of
CHRISTMAS,
O R,
His Twelve Yeares Obfervations upon.the Times, concerning the lamentable Game called Sweep-ftake ; acted by General *Plunder*, and Major General *Tax*; With his Exhortation to the people; a defcription of that 'oppreffing Ringworm called *Excize*; and the manner how our high and mighty Chriftmas-Ale that formerly would knock down *Hercules*, & trip up the heels of a Giant, ftrook into a deep Confumption with a blow from *Weftminfter*.

Keep out, you come not here,

O Sir, I bring good cheere.

Old Chriftmas welcome; Do not fear.

Imprinted at London for G. Horton, 1653.

Few things proved so unpopular as the Puritan ban on the celebration of Christmas as a pagan festival.

their brethren in New England) of the *Apologeticall Narration*, in which they explained their inability to sacrifice the ultimate right of self-determination in particular churches. They would concede the need for supra-parochial synods with authority to admonish and to offer fraternal advice to constituent churches; but not, in the last analysis, to command them. Other differences existed – over the status of elders, for example, and the principle that all communicants should elect the Church officers, but: 'what further authority or proceedings purely ecclesiastical, of one or many sister churches towards another whole Church

Westminster Assembly

From the early days of the Long Parliament, it was widely assumed that the future shape of the national Church would be determined by an assembly of divines or ministers. Plans were laid for it in 1641, but the deteriorating political situation and Charles's unwillingness to endorse such an assembly caused a two-year delay before it finally met in the late summer of 1643. There were to be two clergy from each county (nominated by those MPs from each county who were still sitting), plus two representatives from each university and four from the city of London. Almost all those chosen were veteran preachers and ministers and almost all were university graduates (many had taken higher degrees and had held college fellowships). Several of them had recently returned from exile, but they might have been balanced by the former bishops and moderate episcopalians who were nominated but who tended to stay away. A large proportion had strong links with powerful figures in one or both Houses of Parliament. Altogether there were 90 ministers nominated, together with 30 lay 'assessors'. Scots were added after the signing of the Solemn League and Covenant.

The assembly met frequently over the next four years: they were able to achieve a consensus for the major series of doctrinal and liturgical documents discussed on p.00; but they were increasingly and bitterly divided on questions of Church government. About three-quarters favoured a Presbyterian form of government (although only 26 supported a specifically Scottish pattern), and they were able to present a majority report to Parliament in 1646, only to see it fundamentally revised, especially by the increase of lay control at all levels.

or churches offending, either the scriptures do hold forth, . . . for our parts we saw not then, nor do yet see'.

This tract was seen by many as a brazen betrayal of the very oath they had all recently sworn under the Solemn League and Covenant, by which the English and Scots had bound themselves to extirpate popery and prelacy and to create a single form of Church government in both kingdoms, consonant with 'the word of God and the example of the best reformed Churches'. A majority of the Puritan ministers, and all the Scots, had assumed that this was nothing less than a commitment to introduce classical Presbyterianism.

Urged on by the Scottish delegates to the Assembly, leading ministers anathematized the Apologeticall brethren and their friends. Many Congregationalists stayed on in the Church, refusing to co-operate with the newly-established classes and provinces that were set up in the later 1640s. It proved very difficult to dislodge them, because they frequently enjoyed the patronage of powerful figures on local committees or in the Army. Indeed there were ministers committed to the Independent way in almost a quarter of the London parishes in the mid-1640s. Many of them defiantly set up their own 'churches

Presbyterians and Independents

Throughout the 1640s these are the terms that characterize the two main religious groupings which emerged in the debates on the future shape of the national Church within the Parliamentarian movement in the 1640s. The Presbyterians formed a clear majority of those ministers who were enthusiastic supporters of godly reformation and of perhaps three-quarters of the regular attenders at the Westminster Assembly. They looked to Geneva for inspiration and to Scotland for an example of Church government. They wanted a strict uniformity of faith and practice, and sought to create structures to achieve this end. Each parish was to send ministers and lay elders (elected by all who had taken the Covenant) to local assemblies known as *classes*, which in turn would send representatives to a provincial assembly (one for each county). At the top of the structure would be national assemblies of laymen (Parliament) and of ministers and elders (National Synod). Agreed formularies of faith, rules of worship and codes of moral law would be strictly and uniformly enforced within this national and authoritarian structure. This rigidity still allowed for quite sharp differences amongst the Presbyterians about the precise responsibilities of each 'layer' of Church government.

The Independents were made up of a minority of ministers supported by a growing number of laymen, and they drew inspiration from the churches of New England and from those who had experienced exile in the Netherlands. Their fundamental principles included an insistence upon the sovereignty of each congregation in all matters of faith and practice. Local, regional and national bodies could exist to help co-ordinate evangelism and to provide fraternal counsel and advice, but no minister could exercise any jurisdiction except over his own congregation. They were wary of the open elections of lay elders and advocated that the minister should choose the elders who would then govern with him. The experience of many 'Puritan' parishes before the war made the laity in particular more sympathetic to Independency. Independents always strenuously denied being separatists. They sought to make all people worship and learn their duty to God, but they also emphasized – divisively – the right of the self-consciously and experienced godly to additional and special privileges within the Church. The terms Presbyterian and Independent were casually used by some contemporaries and many historians to denote political groupings or parties in the years 1645–8. It is important to realize that when used in this sense, nothing should be assumed about the religious views of those being discussed. (See information box on p.91.)

within churches', gathering around them and offering additional services to a closed group of like-minded men and women while continuing to serve out a public ministry to the community as a whole and refusing to acknowledge the existence of the Presbyterian classes established by the Parliament. But the schism of the mid-1640s drove many of those who had originally believed strongly in a national Church in the form of a free federation of semi-autonomous Churches to opt for secession, and to swell the number (and crucially the number in positions of power and influence) who were demanding liberty for tender consciences (i.e. toleration) outside the national Church. And this in turn brought the wrath of the Presbyterians down upon their head. 'Liberty of conscience' Thomas Case preached to the House of Commons in 1647 'may in time improve to liberty of estates and houses and wives, and in a word, liberty of perdition of souls and bodies'. The events of the year that followed did nothing to allay his paranoia.

As if this was not enough, a second rift opened up within the majority Presbyterian ranks. For when the Long Parliament received the report of the Westminster Assembly, with its recommendations for the establishment of a Presbyterian order, it decided to change it. What worried many members of the Long Parliament was the rigid separation of the responsibilities and powers of ministers and laymen, and they set out to adjust the balance so as to increase the involvement of lay elders in such crucial areas as the exercise of powers of excommunication. Just as bad was the transfer of ultimate determination of matters of faith and practice from national synods to national Parliaments. The Scots and their English friends were outraged at this blurring of what was for them a crucial and Christ-given distinction of roles.

These rifts were to prove fatal to the introduction of the new system. Under legislation approved in 1646–7, commissioners in each county and in the city of London were to draw up proposals for dividing their county into 'classes', each comprising about eight to sixteen parishes. These classes, the English equivalent of the Scottish presbyteries, would be the primary agencies of ecclesiastical administration and control, confirming ministerial appointments, ordaining ministers, and ensuring orthodox teaching and practice. Internal dissension, the chaos of the post-war period (those nominated as commissioners had 1001 other jobs to do), political disappointment, the collapse of political will at the centre with the Army's seizure of power in the summer of 1647, and sheer disappointment producing a lassitude of the spirit, all led to a very patchy implementation of the new plan. Schemes were generated in only 16 of the 40 English counties; classes were actually up and running by 1649 in parts of ten of those counties, but provincial synods and fairly complete classical systems were effective only in London, Lancashire and Essex. Elsewhere, in the absence of anything else, the parish clergy, often under strong community pressure, were operating various diluted versions of the old religion or else they were practising *de facto* congregationalist worship.

Not surprisingly in this climate, there was a massive spread of unauthorized religious practice outside the parish system. In a later essay, Ian Gentles discusses the development of free worship in the New Model Army. Wherever the Army bivouacked or wherever disbanded soldiers settled, their values would spread. The collapse of the Church courts and the general vacuum of the 1640s lent themselves to the freedom of itinerant preachers (often self-educated laymen) to gather followers around them. The austere preaching of orthodox Calvinist preachers may have had one particular effect: it may have raised the threshold of anxiety and fear of damnation amongst an impressionable population without offering any comfortable expectation of salvation. The Puritan preacher would present as the stereotype of the men and women whom God had predestined to salvation those who knew their scriptures, devoted themselves to a life of strict observance and displayed their saving faith in acts of charity. This offered little to the illiterate man or woman who had neither the leisure nor the resources to

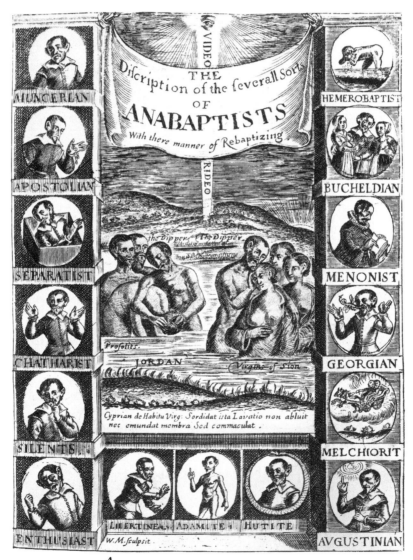

As the 1640s proceeded, so did the controversies about the spread of sects.

live a model life. Such people, with a heightened fear of damnation, could either turn back to the comforting openness of the pre-war Church, or could respond to those anti-Calvinist populist preachers who offered the hope of salvation to all those who opened their hearts to a Christ who came to them mediated not through priestcraft nor even through the scriptures, but rather through the indwelling spirit.

The 1640s saw a great revolt within Puritanism against Calvinist predestinarianism. Intellectuals like John Milton, radical laymen like William Walwyn, and ministers like John Goodwin took advantage of the collapse of censorship to challenge the hitherto all-prevailing and gloomy view of the intellectual and moral depravity of Man, whose nature was so flawed that no individual could *earn* any merit with God. Calvin's severe doctrine arose from the belief that all men and women *deserved* to be damned; God had chosen to redeem some people from a warranted damnation despite their unworthiness. In the course of the 1640s it was this gloomy view of the human condition which was challenged. Man was capable of responding, imperfectly but sufficiently, to the revealed will of God so as to warrant salvation. This idea often led, as it did with the Leveller leaders for example, to the further belief that all men and women should be free to develop their own response to God's revealed will in their own way. The Levellers believed that the most fundamental and inalienable of all human rights was the right to liberty of conscience and almost all their political thought was designed to ensure that no future state could interfere with the exercise of that inalienable right in the way monarchical regimes had done, and corrupt Parliamentary regimes sought to do. Others in the later 1640s went further still. Jacob Bauthumley, a New Model Quartermaster and lay preacher sometimes described as a 'Ranter' went too far even for the advocates of religious liberty in the army in 1650: he was cashiered and had his tongue bored with a red hot iron in front of his comrades for claiming that God suffused every created thing, and that the struggle between *the Light and Dark Sides of God* (to quote the title of his only published tract) was taking place within every breast. His message could not have owed less to the Reformation: 'I do not expect to be taught by Bibles or Books, but by God . . . if men were acted and guided by that inward law of righteousness within, there need be no laws of men, to compel or restrain men, and I could wish that such a spirit of righteousness would appear, that men did not act or do things from external rules . . .'

For most of those who in 1641 had seen themselves in the process of building a New Jerusalem in England; of perfecting the institutions of Church and state so as to perfect the nation's knowledge of and obedience to the will of God, the 1640s were a decade of heartbreak and disillusionment. In 1641, preachers could confidently assert that even if Christ's second coming was imminent, they had work to do:

> In the meantime we may yet enjoy a summer of the gospel and a harvest of a better Reformation . . . Christ knew he was to be crucified yet he casts the money changers out of the Temple; and so do you purge and reform the Temple . . . Be strong and of good courage, fear not nor be dismayed, for the Lord God will be with thee, he will not fail thee, nor forsake thee, until thou hast finished the work for the service of the house of the Lord . . .

By 1644, the same metaphor is being used but in a more guarded way:

> At the building of a royal palace, where much rubbish is to be removed by many hands, where timber, stones and other materials are to be brought together and set in the work by a multitude of divers craftsmen, no marvel if in that place for a time there be much noise and stir, much commotion, and some confusions . . . The ordering of the state and kingdom, how necessary soever, ought not to precede the setting up of the Church.

Reassurance not exhilaration was by now the hallmark.

By 1649, for most of those who had set out to erect the Temple, to build Zion, to impose order, the cause was lost. In 1648, many of these men were fighting for the King in the second Civil War, or were voting, as the majority of MPs did on 3 December 1648, for his restoration on terms that offered no guarantee against a return to the past. Most 'Puritans' deplored the regicide, were never to reconcile themselves to the Interregnum regimes, and would become conforming Anglicans in the Restoration Church. Only a tiny minority embraced the chaos of the later 1640s as God-given, part of God's plan. Pre-eminent amongst those who embraced the challenge of the collapse of Protestant unity, who welcomed the challenge of diversity, was Oliver Cromwell. He could exhort his friends to trust in God, to let all human forms dissolve to be modelled anew by God in his own good time. Few shared his confidence or his vision. Even his own chaplain, John Owen, preaching to the Rump of the Long Parliament the day after Cromwell's death, was using building metaphors in a distinctly downbeat way. He preached on the text 'I will make thee unto this people a fenced, brazen wall; and they shall fight against thee, but they shall not prevail.' He said:

> All you, then, that are the Lord's workmen, be always prepared for a storm. Wonder not that men see not the ways of the Lord nor the judgments of our God . . . But this do: come and enter into the chambers of God, and you shall safe until this whole indignation be overpast . . . Be prepared, the wind blows – a storm may come

If this was where Puritan rhetoric had moved between 1641 and 1649, it is not surprising that the 1650s proved not a journey across the Desert to the Promised land, but a dispirited trek back to Egypt.

CHAPTER IV

The Impact on Political Thought: Rhetorics for Troubled Times

GLENN BURGESS

The English Civil War was the first European civil war to be fought within a society that possessed a well-established culture of the vernacular printed word. Earlier civil wars, most notably the French Wars of Religion, did have their accompanying propaganda battles, but on nothing like the scale of England in the 1640s. It is this combination of civil war with pamphleteering that has made the English Civil War look more like the first great European revolution than it really was. All the same, to understand the decade of the Civil War we must confront the battle of the printing presses as fully as we confront the battle of the armies.

Historians have usually analysed the political thought contained in pamphlets of the 1640s in broadly philosophical terms. This has involved exploring the philosophical bases for arguments about the right of subjects to resist their King (or their duty to obey him), philosophical theories about the nature of political representation, theories about the sources and origins of political authority, the philosophy of mixed monarchy, and so on. Yet, arguably, any such approach to the subject is inherently distorting. The debaters and pamphleteers of the 1640s were arguing to a political brief, and were less interested in philosophical underpinnings than in ideological consequences. Indeed, they took pride in being able to use their opponents' philosophy for their own ends. To counter a conquering King one might look to a conquering army. If Henry Parker could speak of Parliament as the absolute embodiment of popular consent, then Thomas Hobbes could speak of sovereign kings in the same way. This was a decade when the need to argue a case prevailed over first principles. It was, in short, an age of political persuasion, of *rhetoric*, rather than an age of political philosophy. It needs to be understood as such.

This involves us in a consideration not just of the philosophical theories that people employed, but also of their attempts to *persuade* an audience that they had right on their side. Pamphleteers were not always too fussy about how they achieved this. On all sides attempts were made to exploit shared 'rhetorics'. These 'rhetorics' were not ideologies or political doctrines; they were arguments of persuasion that both (or all) sides utilized as best they could. The history of political debate in the England of the Civil War is best written in terms of these 'rhetorics', of attempts by various political groups to exploit the available conventions of argument; and sometimes of the consequences of a failure to exploit them successfully.

Three rhetorics were central to the 1640s (though others can also be found): the rhetoric of counsel; the rhetoric of peace and moderation; and the rhetoric of 'Godly Rule'. Through these rhetorics Englishmen in the 1640s attempted, not just to understand, but to control and regulate the impact of the Civil War on their lives and communities. Rhetorics were weapons rather than ideas. Pamphleteers in the 1640s were not passively reacting to the impact of events; they were creating and moulding them.

The rhetoric of counsel and its problems

When the Long Parliament first met in November 1640, few of its members would have contemplated the possibility of overt resistance to or rebellion against their King. Yet, before the end of 1642 some of them had, at least in the King's eyes, become rebels. But those Parliamentarians fighting the King remained unwilling to see themselves as rebels or resisters. Instead they preferred to characterize themselves as counsellors, and their actions as attempts to make an obdurately wrong-headed king take the advice of his proper advisers. It was, they thought, much more persuasive to pose as a *loyal* counsellor than to pose as a lawless destroyer of established authority.

Throughout the 1640s it remained a constant feature of the settlement proposals offered by Parliament to the King that they attempted to control tightly those who might have the right or opportunity to give counsel to the monarch in the future. The Nineteen Propositions were not so much a request for 'Parliamentary sovereignty' as a request that the King seek counsel only from those fit to give it [see David Smith's chapter 'The impact on government', pp. 00–00 and information box 1]. This remained a central war aim of the Parliamentarians and their later peace proposals all sought to spell out in great detail who would be allowed to counsel the King. Particular groups and individuals were to be 'removed from His Majesty's counsels, and restrained from coming within the verge of the Court'. In an era of personal monarchy, access to the court was a more pressing concern than the question of where sovereignty lay.

This emphasis on the need to ensure that the King was counselled by those who would counsel most wisely, was reflected in the rhetoric through which Parliamentarians presented their cause. This was most apparent in the first years of the Civil War. In these years Parliamentarian propaganda portrayed Charles as a man led astray by 'evil counsellors'; and portrayed their own actions as those of loyal men acting in *defence* of the King. Charles Herle, in 1642, claimed that

> a Parliament of England may with good conscience, in defence of *King, Lawes,* and *Government* establisht, when imminently endangered, especially when actually invaded, take up Armes without and against the *Kings* personall Commands, if he refuse.

In September 1643 members of the House of Commons took the Solemn League and Covenant in which they further affirmed their aim 'to preserve and defend the King's Majesty's person and authority'. Those fighting the King were loyal counsellors fighting to be listened to. Could it be said, Herle wanted to know, that the papists who flocked to the King's banner were 'better Subjects then those of his great Councell?'

'Resistance' was easier to defend under another name; it was easier to defend as the substitution of good counsel for bad. Philip Hunton, in May 1643 was able to conclude

That the two Houses may lawfully resist by force of Armes, all counsells and attempts of what men soever tending to the subversion of the established Frame of Government or themselves and their Fundamentall Priviledges

Such action was 'no resistance of the higher power' so long as 'no force be intended or used against the Kings owne Person'. The crucial point is that much so-called resistance theory of the early 1640s was actually the rhetorical denial that resistance to *lawful* authority had occurred. Even the most discussed of all Parliamentarian tracts, Henry Parker's *Observations upon some of his Majesties late Answers and Expresses* (1642), averred that 'the maine question now is, whether the Court or the Parliament gives the King the better Councell'. Parker's

---

Resistance Theory

In England during the 1640s Parliament's rebellion against the King was often defended with reference to *resistance theories* of a sort first developed in sixteenth-century Scotland and France. The theory was given its fullest elaboration prior to the 1640s in the writings of French Huguenots of the 1570s. Because the theory had generally been used to defend the resistance of Calvinist minorities against their rulers, it has come to be called the Calvinist theory of resistance. In fact, much of its theoretical basis was first developed by late medieval Catholic writers. In the writings of Parliamentarian propagandists of the first Civil War (1642–6) many of the classic statements of the Calvinist theory of resistance were referred to, including works by Buchanan, Ponet, Beza, Hotman, and the anonymous Huguenot tract known as the *Vindiciae contra Tyrannos*. Nevertheless, the English writers did not simply copy the ideas of their sixteenth-century predecessors. They used them creatively, often combining them with native English ideas such as those attached to the common law.

The Calvinist theory of resistance had two characteristic components. First, it was a *populist* theory which argued that the entire community (acting as a collective unit) had chosen its own rulers, and had given them authority, and retained the right to take action should the ruler use such authority in a tyrannical fashion. For many the community had a *duty* to take action against a King who broke the laws of God by favouring false religion. The second distinctive feature of the theory, especially in its French forms, was that it was a theory of *lesser magistrates*. For though the people had a collective right to resist a tyrant, it was generally thought that this right could not be exercised by any individual but only on the initiative of lesser magistrates. These people were those who held public office beneath the King. In England during the 1640s some, like the Levellers, began to play around with the idea that individuals too had rights of resistance that they could exercise on their own initiative. But even Levellers remained highly tentative on this matter.

[167]

(1)

OBSERVATIONS

upon some of his Majesties late *An-*
fwers and *Expreffes.*

The second Edition corrected from some groffe errors in the Preffe.

N this conteftation betweene Regall and Paliamentary power, for methods fake it is requifite to confider firft of Regall, then of Parliamentary Power, and in both to confider the efficient, and finall caufes, and the meanes by which they are fupported. *The King attributeth the originall of his royalty to God, and the Law, making no mention of the graunt, confent, or truft of man therein,* but the truth is, God is no more the author of Regall, then of Ariftocraticall power, nor of fupreame, then of fubordinate command; nay, that dominion which is ufurped, and not juft, yet whilft it remaines dominion, and till it be legally againe devefted, referres to God, as to its Author and donor, as much as that which is hereditary. *And that Law which the King mentioneth, is not to be underftood to be any fpeciall ordinance fent from heaven by the miniftery of Angels or Prophets (as amongft the Jewes it fometimes was)* It can be nothing elfe amongft Chriftians but the Pactions and agreements of fuch and fuch politique corporations. Power is originally inherent in the people, and it is nothing elfe but that might and vigour which fuch or fuch a focietie of men containes in it felfe, and when by fuch or fuch a Law of common confent and agreement it is derived into fuch and fuch hands, God confirmes that Law : and fo man is the free and voluntary Author, the Law is the Inftrument, and God is the eftablifher of both. And we fee, net that Prince which

A   is

Henry Parker's Observations *was the most influential of Parliamentarian propagandist tracts of 1642.*

arguments for Parliament as the embodiment of the people's rights was designed in part to buttress his portrayal of the Parliamentarian cause as an attempt by loyal men to perform their duty of giving counsel. Kings should act neither on 'their owne private advise' nor on the advice of 'privadoes', for 'publick advise be commonly better than private'. In Parker's portrayal, the Parliament was not really resisting, but acting as an emergency court capable of judging when the 'seducement' of the king by private advisers needed to be checked. Parliament had that role because it represented the essence of the whole kingdom, and had an absolute power to exercise the people's rights over themselves. In 1642 Parker covered the radical implications of these latter arguments with his portrait of the King's opponents as loyal counsellors.

In any history of rhetorics attention must be paid to the consequences of the failure or inability of people to employ the rhetoric of their choice with much success. The measure of success, of course, is how well the task of persuasion (usually of persuading a particular audience) is actually performed. The success or failure of rhetorical positions is no doubt partially dependent on an ability to ensure that one's rhetorical acts were not too far out of line with one's other actions. This was the problem encountered in the 1640s by those rebels who wished to persuade themselves and others that they were really counsellors. The development of theories of resistance to monarchy in England was perhaps just part of the story of the collapse of a rhetoric of counsel.

In their important *Declaration* of 21 March 1649 a now much-reduced Commons roundly, if a little opaquely, declared that:

> the same power and authority which first erected a king, and made him a public officer for the common good, finding him perverted to the common calamity, it may justly be admitted, at the pleasure of those whose officer he is, whether they will continue that officer any longer, or change that government for a better; and instead of restoring tyranny, to resolve into a free state.

It was, of course, scarcely possible to argue that cutting off the King's head was a way of giving him counsel, and so it is not surprising to see that defence of regicide required of Parliamentarians a rather different rhetorical position. They chose (on 21 March 1649, at any rate) to emphasize their role as representatives of the people, 'intrusted and authorized by the consent of all the people . . . whose Representatives, by election, they are'. When forced openly to defend resistance to the King, or even regicide, Parliamentarians did so by arguing that they were the unquestionable embodiment of popular consent, able to exercise whatever force was necessary to save the kingdom from destruction. Yet, even in 1649, the Commons did not forget that its struggles began as an attempt to give counsel to their monarch: they patiently explained that as late as 1646 they had wished to make Charles a 'great and happy prince', believing that 'the King's ill counsel once removed from him, he would have conformed himself to the Desires of his people in Parliament'.

The roots of this position enunciated in 1649 go right back to 1642. The inadequacy of the rhetoric of counsel arose in part from the fact that repeated negotiations with the King eventually made some in the army and the Commons realize that they would need to be more than counsellors if they wished to sway the mind of Charles Stuart. This led to the search for other rhetorical stances that might accommodate taking a less supine attitude before the King. Until Pride's Purge on 6 December 1648 those seeking these alternatives were a minority, most members of the Commons wishing to continue negotiation with the King. Which is to say that most wished to remain counsellors. But for the minority who did not want negotiations to continue, a central concern was the portrayal of Parliamentarianism as being concerned with the welfare of the people, *salus populi*; and of themselves as the representatives of the people. In the *Declaration of the Parliament of England, in Vindication of their Proceedings* (28 September 1649) the victorious party showed some awareness of the changing tactical stances that they had taken, but asserted also that 'Religion in its purity, and public Liberty, were the ends which, from the beginning, we had before our eyes when we engaged in this great Work'. The ends of liberty and true religion remained constant, though the means necessary to pursue them had changed over the 1640s. Oliver Cromwell, writing in November 1648, raised the possibility that the army's justification in these years lay not in the fact that its power was delegated to it by a lawful Parliament, but rather in the rightness of the ends it pursued: 'it was not the outward Authority summoning them that by *its* power made the quarrel lawful, but the quarrel was lawful in itself'. Those ends that made the quarrel lawful in itself were religion and liberty, together constituting the good of the people. And as John Goodwin explained in *Right and Might Well Met* (1649), those acting for the people (whether army or Parliament) might do so 'without the particular and express consent, but even contrary to the mind and desires of the people, or at least of the major part of them'. The people's good was an objective thing, not something to be determined by asking people what they wanted. Thus Parliament (or the army) was the representative of the people not just (sometimes not at all) because it derived its authority from them, but also because it was pursuing their welfare.

Thus by the end of the 1640s tiny minorities were able to use 'resistance theory' to justify their actions as the work of the people. To modern eyes this looks self-contradictory, since we tend to read 'the people' in a democratic way. But it made perfect sense in 1648 to think that the people's interests were not necessarily served by giving *all* of the people power. Most of them would only use it to pursue ends harmful to themselves and others. What mattered in the 1640s was not who held authority but the purposes for which it was used. Charles's opponents were not, at first, opponents of monarchy: they wished to see themselves as counsellors urging the King to follow *the* right path. When they defended resistance to the King they did so initially not because they thought that 'the people' (meaning usually small groups acting in the name of the people) could alter their form of government as they liked. Indeed, a King who governed with the right ends in sight *was* irresistible, and only a King who attacked the common good by refusing to recognize true religion or infringing the liberties of his subjects, could be resisted. Even here there were limits. John Milton, defending the regicide in his pamphlet *The Tenure of Kings and Magistrates* (1649), was forced to rebut the arguments of one of the most influential early defences of the Parliamentarian position. This was a pamphlet issued in 1643 by the London Puritan ministers, *Scripture and Reason pleaded for Defensive Armes*, which argued, as did most others, that resistance

Sir Thomas Fairfax
Knight, Captain-Generall
of the Parliaments Forces.

After the fighting was over, it was military men who sought to dictate the peace.

was for defence only. Once the King's excesses were curbed he would remain King and had to be obeyed in all lawful things.

The fundamental issues of the 1640s were not about the nature or extent of authority but about its right employment. Charles's opponents were as interested as he was in securing the obedience of people to what they considered just commands. The rhetoric of counsel became inadequate to deal with the situation not when war broke out in 1642 (as late as 1646 Parliament was still talking of removing evil counsellors and making their own counsel effective). It became

73

finally inadequate when men could no longer be certain that just counselling a King would actually ensure that he pursued godly and just things. This point came at different times for different people, for Henry Parker by 1643, for Oliver Cromwell perhaps not until late in 1648. When men could no longer be content with portraying themselves as loyal counsellors, they tended instead to portray themselves as either popular representatives or agents (tools, perhaps) of divine providence. Parliament in 1649, for example did both, taking up the first stance in its March *Declaration*, and the second in September. Oliver Cromwell in 1648 debated (with himself, as usual) whether the army might be considered to be effectively the representative of the people, but decided that 'this kind of reasonings may be but fleshly' and that more importance should be placed on the record of 'providences' which had been 'so constant, so clear, unclouded'. Both images, acting for the people or acting for God, were of some appeal, and both could support the actions of men prepared to do everything they believed to be required of them. The important thing for those who chose to portray themselves as counsellors, the people's representative, or God's vassal, was that the role in which they cast themselves must be one that enabled them to *act* for religion and liberty.

Rhetorics of peace and moderation

Not everyone in the 1640s wanted to choose a rhetorical stance that would give them a *public* role. Indeed, it was a widespread assumption in early modern thinking that private persons ought to have no public function. Those who held public office might have some role in political life; the rest of the population were to do no more than obey their rulers. If such private citizens took it upon themselves to acquire public political roles, the only consequence would be disorder. For many, the events of the 1640s bore this out all too vividly. Even those who might sympathize with the objectives of one side or the other in the conflicts, might deplore the consequences of war, and desire peace. There was then substantial rhetorical appeal to be derived from the claim that one was a peacemaker, or from the pose of 'moderation' which made one out to be someone who was not trying to increase disorder. Proposals could win support if they were advanced as a plan for settlement and peace. Many chose to avail themselves of such a rhetorical stance.

The first obvious effect of the attractiveness of a rhetoric of moderation was the Royalist adoption of mixed monarchy theory. The story behind Charles I's use of this theory in his *Answer to the xix propositions* (1642) is an immensely complicated one. In England the idea that the constitution was a mixed one, in which the three estates (King, lords and commons) balanced each other, had been used from 1640 by the opponents of Charles and of episcopacy. But by 1642 the theory had become of most use to Royalists. Significantly, the first sign of this happening was in a pamphlet published in April 1642 and called *A plea for moderation*. Then, later in the year, the *Answer* appeared in which Charles portrayed himself as a peaceful moderate. The benefit of mixed government was that it joined the advantages of monarchy, aristocracy and democracy together 'as long as the balance hangs even between the three estates, and they run jointly on in their proper channel'. The balancing effect of the other two estates automatically prevented monarchy from degenerating into tyranny. Thus it would be ensured 'that the prince may not make use of this high and perpetual power to the hurt of those for whose good he hath it'. In other words, Charles was telling his subjects that they could safely trust him as he was powerless to do anything to their harm. [See also the discussion in David Smith's chapter 'The impact on government', p. 45 and information box 2.]

The language of mixture and balance employed in the *Answer* remained central to the rhetorics of peaceful moderation throughout the 1640s. Though the use of this approach by Charles has been considered by some historians to have been a tactical mistake, this is probably not true. The rhetorical advantages in being on the side of peace and moderation outweighed any theoretical disadvantages of mixed monarchy theory. Certainly, the theory could be employed by Parliamentarians as well as Royalists, but it remained a staple of Royalist propaganda in spite of this fact (although explicit discussion of the three *estates* tended to fade from view after the early 1640s).

Philip Hunton in *A Treatise of Monarchie* (May 1643) presented himself as a searcher after 'the readiest meanes of Reconcilement', someone who wrote not 'to foment or heighten the wofull dissention of the Kingdome; but if possible to cure, or at least to allay it'. In the body of his book Hunton portrayed the

---

Mixed Monarchy Theory and the Estates of the Realm

In the early 1640s it was widely believed that the English constitution was a *mixed monarchy*. Some went further and analysed mixed monarchy in terms of the *three estates*. These two ideas are in origin separate. Mixed monarchy theory developed from the Renaissance idea that the most stable form of government was a mixture of the three 'good' forms identified by the Greeks, monarchy, aristocracy, and democracy. From the sixteenth century onwards some identified this as the English pattern, whereby supreme authority resided in the King-in-Parliament. There was thus a fusion of monarchy (the King), aristocracy (House of Lords) and democracy (House of Commons).

The idea of the three estates began as a way of describing feudal society (those who fight, those who pray, those who work), and thus it originally was defined as lords temporal (the first estate), lords spiritual or bishops (the second estate), and commoners (the third estate). However as Presbyterians began to attack episcopacy in the late sixteenth century they found, for tactical reasons, an advantage in denying that bishops formed one of the estates of the realm, and so the three estates became King, lords and commons. This language was revived when bishops were attacked in Scotland in 1638, and again in the Long Parliament for similar reasons. There was at this time a temporary propaganda advantage to be derived from using the language of the three estates to describe a mixed monarchy, but it was at best an unstable alliance of two separate ideas. While the theory of mixed monarchy continued to play an important role in the 1640s, the idea of the three estates did not.

English monarchy as a mixed, limited monarchy. But he concluded that if, in such a constitution, the parts of the mixture (King, lords and commons) fell out amongst themselves, there was no legal mechanism that could judge between their competing claims. In this unhappy state the individual might be left with only his or her own conscience as a guide for deciding where their loyalties lay. But Hunton closed his work by reverting to his stance of mediator and peacemaker. He put forward five points on which he hoped a settlement would be possible. They appear to have been genuinely moderate, seeking to avoid the excesses of both sides. Parliament was asked to seek only things necessary for the preservation of public safety, while the King was asked to consent to such measures as were compatible with fundamental law. Parliament was advised, also, that it should seek retribution only against those evil advisers who were responsible for the initial drive towards arbitrary rule, and not to confuse them with the entire body of those fighting on the Royalist side.

The King's most prominent early defender, Henry Ferne, replied to Hunton in November 1643. Though historians have given some attention to the different constitutional theories of the two writers, it is just as important to note that they were (in propaganda terms) involved in a battle for moderation. Substantially they *agreed* in their portrayals of English monarchy. For both of them Kings of England were legally limited, that is they were limited not just by the laws of God and nature but by civil laws too. In Ferne's words: there is 'a Legall restraint upon the Power of the Monarch in this Kingdome'. Ferne agreed also that England was a mixed monarchy, though in his view the lords and commons had gained their place in the legislative process by the King's grace. Nevertheless, once the King had granted them such a role he could not take it away again. The area in dispute between Hunton and Ferne was primarily the implications of the idea that English monarchy was limited and not arbitrary. Ferne was adamant that the legal limits on kings were not enforceable by their subjects. Kings were limited but also irresistible.

In rhetorical terms the Royalists had a strong case to make. Try as he might to sound moderate, Hunton's reliance upon individual consciences was an alarming one. In general, as we have seen, Parliamentarian rhetoric was increasingly activist, portraying adherents to the cause as men with a justifiable public role to play. Ferne was quick to call this 'a ready way to Anarchy and confusion'. Royalist rhetoric had an easier task: it did not need to cut against the grain of seventeenth-century assumptions. Parliamentarian rhetoric always tended to be in tension with itself. The rhetoric was conservative, moderate, anti-innovationary (on the whole); yet it needed also to justify a public active role for private men, contrary to the King's commands. The best they could do to bridge the gap was to rely on a theory of 'lesser magistrates', which allowed subordinate officials and officers (like Members of Parliament) to join together to moderate the excesses of their superior. Essentially, lesser magistrates were counsellors who would not take no for an answer. But as, in the later 1640s, it became apparent that Charles would not be moderated or counselled, Parliamentary rhetoric became increasingly dependent on the activism inherent in popular representatives and agents of providence. Royalists were always able to play on the theme of the threat to peace, the fundamental lack of moderation, in the positions taken by their Parliamentarian opponents.

Thus, though our attention might be focused on the new and exciting ideas produced by the King's opponents, we should not lose sight of the fact that very probably Royalist propaganda would have had a greater natural appeal to the political nation of the 1640s. But the themes of peace, and withdrawal from public life, were not confined to them. During 1645 in a number of counties in the south and west local Clubmen Associations were formed. The Clubmen were groups of peasants who came together ready to use force to preserve their local communities from the ravages of Royalist and Parliamentarian troops. They seem on the whole not to have taken a stand on the issues that divided the King from his enemies, though they were prepared to make tactical alliances with one side or another. The central theme of the petitions and statements of the Clubmen was the threat to their liberties posed by Civil War. In July 1645 the Wiltshire Clubmen petitioned the King, telling him how deeply they had 'tasted the Miseries of this unnatural intestine War'. They hoped for a settlement that

> may prove for the Advancement of God's glory in the Maintenance of the true
> Reformed Protestant Religion, for the Safeguard of Your Majesty's Royal Person,
> Honour and Estate, for the securing of the Privileges and Immunities of Parliament,
> and for the Preservation of the Liberties and Properties of the Subject.

The real interest of the Clubmen lay as much in what followed, the demand for local control over the troops in their area, and the hope that those active in the Civil War would be able to return to civilian life unhindered. Their desire was, in short, for a return to the things they had before the Civil War, and which were being threatened by both of the contending armies.

While the Clubmen, with their attention fixed on their local communities, could see both Royalists and Parliamentarians as threats to liberty and property, Royalists exploited the same potent theme in a more ideologically pointed fashion. From 1642 to 1649 a constant theme of Royalist thought was the threat to liberty and property posed by the rebellion of the King's subjects. This view was given classic expression by Charles himself in the statement he gave (21 January 1649) of his reasons for refusing to recognize the jurisdiction of the High Court of Justice set up to try him:

> Thus you see that I speak not for my own right alone, as I am your King,
> but also for the true liberty of all my subjects, which consists not in the power
> of government, but in living under such laws, such a government, as may give
> themselves the best assurance of their lives, and property of their goods.

How could those who would deny to the King his liberty and property be expected to defend the property of anyone else? In an age in which liberties and rights were conceived as a form of property, and were thought to be defined by the law, this was a worrying question indeed. It was so worrying that John Lilburne, the Leveller leader, agreed with the King on this point: the regicide was an arbitrary act that threatened the legal rights of everybody.

So, while before 1642 the King's actions (above all the imposition of ship-money) were said to be arbitrary acts of government threatening his subjects' peaceful enjoyment of their property, by the end of the 1640s this situation had reversed. The Parliamentarian war effort required military government and financial exactions to a far greater degree than anything seen in the 1620s or 1630s. Royalist rhetoric played on this theme increasingly. The most notable Royalist writer and theorist of the later 1640s was the Welshman Judge David Jenkins. His major work, which appeared in 1647, was called *Lex Terrae*, and it is significant that Jenkins chose to place the weight of his case on the laws of the land rather than the rights of the King. The book was a detailed analysis of the illegalities committed by Parliament. Jenkins emphasised that the King had remedied by Act of Parliament all the grievances of which he was accused during 1641. Since then Parliament had broken all the laws that they had accused the King of violating, and more besides. The case was powerfully and eloquently argued. 'Without the King and the Lawes, you will never have one hour of safety for your Persons, Wives, Children or Estates.' Jenkins had a strong case and this enabled him, from a position of strength, to pose as a peace-loving moderate: he proposed as a basis for settlement an Act of Oblivion, the payment of arrears to soldiers, and allowance to be made for tender consciences.

Radicalism and the rhetoric of 'Godly Rule'

While Royalists increasingly concentrated on portraying themselves as defenders of order, peace and law (all of which required an acceptance of subjection), from another direction the threats to these things were becoming alarmingly prominent. The 1640s saw the development of radical theories and ideas that challenged many of the features of the traditional world. Amongst the things challenged were the clergy's monopoly of spiritual authority, the representative nature of the House of Commons, and even social hierarchy itself. Historians have had great trouble in explaining how these ideas came into existence, and it may help in this matter to view them in rhetorical terms.

One of the features of the language and rhetoric of the radical writers was that it reworked themes first put forward in the propaganda of the Parliamentarians. For example, one Leveller tract of July 1647, Richard Overton's *An Appeale from the Degenerate Representative Body . . . to the Body Represented*, reworked the ideas involved in Parliament's portrayal of itself as the representative of the people. Most Parliamentarians meant by that self-portrayal to indicate that they had an *absolute* right to act on the people's behalf. The people had surrendered their rights to their representatives and had no capacity to exercise them on their own behalf. But from quite early in the 1640s Parliament began to lose control over this rhetorical position as people in the wider political nation started to argue that, just as Parliament could control an erring King, so the people at large could check an erring Parliament. William Ball, writing in 1645, argued that Parliament could be resisted, where it was acting wrongly, by the corporate bodies of the counties and towns of the realm. This idea played a large part in Leveller constitutional theory: the whole idea of an agreement of the people rested on the view that the people as a whole and not just their representatives had an active part to play in the reconstruction of political order. Thus, the rhetoric employed by Parliament was a dangerous thing which always remained a little beyond the secure control of those who employed it. It is little wonder that so many found it rather frightening.

Another example of the same process was Gerrard Winstanley's manipulation of the term 'commonwealth' in 1649 and after. The Rump Parliament called the

[311]

✦✦✦

ENGLANDS LAMENTABLE SLAVERIE,

Proceeding from the Arbitrarie will, severitie, and Injustices of Kings, Negligence, corruption, and unfaithfulnesse of Parliaments, Covetousnesse, ambition, and variablenesse of Priests, and simplicitie, carelesnesse, and cowardlinesse of People.

Which slaverie, with the Remedie may be easily observed.

By the scope of a modest & smooth Letter, written by a true Lover of his Countrey and a faithfull friend to that Worthy Instrument of Englands Freedome, Lievten. Collonell Lilburn, now unjustlie imprisoned in Newgate.

Being committed first, by Order and Vote of Parliament without cause shewed, and then secondly for refusing to answer upon Interrogatories to their Committee of Examinations, Contrarie to

1. The Great Charter of England,
2. The very words of the Petition of right.
3. The Act made this present Parliament; for the abolishing the Star-Chamber.
4. The Solemne Protestation of this Kingdome.
5. And to the great Vow and Covenant for uniting the two Kingdomes together.

The Copie of which Letter (with the Superscription thereof) hereafter followeth.

A private Letter of publique use, to the constant maintainer of the Just Liberties of the People of England, Lievten. Coll. John Lilburn Prisoner in Newgate by command of Parliament.

SIR,   London 1st Octob. 1645

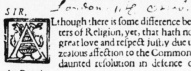

Lthough there is some difference between you and mee in matters of Religion, yet, that hath no white abated in me, that great love and respect justly due unto you, for your constant zealous affection to the Common Wealth, and for your undaunted resolution in defence of the common freedome of the People.

A   The

The title page of an early Leveller tract.

regime that it established after the King's execution a 'commonwealth', probably because this term avoided a specific commitment to republican ideology (though ironically the effect of this was to link the word with republicanism ever after). Commonwealth was a word in common use since the early sixteenth century to express the idea that the whole country formed a single community dedicated to the pursuit of the welfare of all (*salus populi*). It neatly linked the goals expressed in Parliamentary propaganda in the 1640s with traditional ideas of social harmony. Winstanley, however, took this commitment to the establishment of a commonwealth rather differently from the way in which it was intended. The destruction of kingly power would only be accomplished with the destruction of covetousness; hence, the commonwealth would only be established when private ownership of the land was abolished. Until Parliament took that step,

[373]

THE
COMMONERS
COMPLAINT:
OR,
A DREADFVL WARNING
FROM
Newgate, to the Commons of England.

PRESENTED

To the Honourable Committee for confideration of the
Commoners Liberties.

Wherein(as in a Glaffe) every Free-man of *England* may clearly behold
his own imminent infufferable bondage and flavery under the *Nor-*
man-Prerogative Men of this Kingdom, reprefented by the prefent
fufferings of *Richard Overton*; who for his juft Vindicaticn of the
Commoners Rights and Freedoms againft the Arbitrary Domination
of the Houfe of Lords, hath by them bin imprifoned thefe 6 Months
in the Goal of Newgate, his wife and his brother alfo by them moft
unjuftly caft into *Maiden Lane* prifon: And from thence, fhe(with her
tender babe of half a years age in her armes) was, for refufing active
fubjection to their Arbytrary Orders, dragg'd moft barbaroufly and
inhumanely head-long upon the ftones through the ftreets in the dirt
and mire (as was her husband formerly (*Novemb.3.*1646) for the
faid caufe) worfe then Rebels, Traytors, Thieves, or Murtherers,
to the place of execution: And in that moft contemptible and villai-
nous manner caft into the moft reproachful, infamous Goal of Bride-
well : And their 3 fmall children(as helpleffe Orphans bereft of Father and Mother, Sifter and Brother) expofed to the mercy of the
wide world.

Whereunto is annexed the refpective Appeales of his wife, and of his
brother, unto the High Court of Parliament, the Commons of *Eng-*
land affembled at *Weftminfter.*

Ifa. 59. 14. *And judgment is turned backward, and juftice ftandeth a farre*
off : for Truth is fallen in the ftreet, and Equity cannot enter.

Fb: 10th: Printed *Anno Dom.* 1646.

*L*eveller tracts argued that Parliament had come to be as arbitrary as
the King had ever been.

its commitment to the idea of commonwealth was suspect: 'words without action are a cheat'. What neater statement could be imagined of the dangers that its own rhetoric held for Parliament?

So, rhetorical manipulation and rhetorical shift help us to understand much of the language of radicalism. But what we have yet to explain is why Winstanley believed that the destruction of private ownership itself was necessary. If there is one theme that linked together many of the radical writers of the later 1640s (including William Walwyn, Abiezer Coppe and Winstanley himself) it was the belief in the importance of 'practical Christianity'. This theme had its roots in a rhetoric that we have already touched upon. In September 1649 we saw that Parliament justified itself in terms of carrying out God's work. The rhetoric of 'Godly Rule' was present in England from the beginning of the 1640s. It entailed the belief that legitimate government was defined by its capacity to do God's work. This stance was potentially much more radical than any of the other major rhetorical positions used in the 1640s because it had the capacity to overcome the normal seventeenth-century preference for conservation over innovation. It was better to preserve rather than to change things – *unless*, that is, God was active in the world and was himself pulling down established structures. For some, by the late 1640s, providence had shown the inadequacy of King, Parliament and army to serve as agents of God's work. These people found themselves involved in a search for the authority that would do God's work, for the type of rule that would actually enact the commandments of Christ. This seems to have been the main generator of radical theory.

But, again, the basic rhetorical position was not invented by the radicals who employed it. Before the Civil War began the Puritan preachers repeatedly told the members of the House of Commons that they were engaged in God's work of furthering reformation. Throughout the 1640s Parliamentarian propaganda stuck with the rhetoric. In the pamphlet literature, the rhetoric frequently became explicitly millenarian in tone, with the need for the nation's commitment to Christ heightened by the consciousness of living in the last days. As Stephen Marshall put it in 1644, 'the question in England is, whether Christ or Antichrist shall be Lord or King'. This rhetoric was not at first necessarily anti-monarchical. Francis Cheynell talked in 1643 of doing battle *for* the King against the Beast in order that 'the power regained may be settled upon the Kings Royall person, and posterity'.

But even more than the rhetoric of popular representation, this was a language hard to control. Once the claim was made that political activism could be justified by reference to God's cause, it was open to anyone to produce their own view of what God's cause required. This was what the radicals of the later 1640s were doing; and the point they stressed was the need to get beyond rhetoric. Words were not enough: God required deeds. Characteristic in the tracts of writers like Coppe was a blistering attack on hypocrisy and hypocrites, those who used the rhetoric of Godliness without showing their practical commitment to it. Radicalism, then, was more than just the redeployment of Parliamentarian rhetoric. It was the desire to avoid rhetoric altogether, to get to the essences that lay behind words; and as such it looks very different from the complex and intricate casuistry employed by Parliamentarians and Royalists.

These points apply to Levellers, Diggers and others; but perhaps their best exemplification was in the anonymous tract of August 1649, *Tyranipocrit Discovered*. The basic theme was announced near the beginning: 'wee which call our selves Christians, do seeme to exceed all Nations in al manner of impieties'. This was so because, though the English had taken Christ as their law-giver, they did not actually follow the laws he laid down. Central to this problem was the fact that preachers had told people to value faith above love or charity. Following this advice, the rulers of England were not only tyrants but also hypocrites (hence 'tyranipocrit') because they did not practise the gospel that they professed. The social and political message of *Tyranipocrit* was that if the true essence of Christianity (love) was to be institutionalized this would result in a community in which goods were equally distributed. Rulers ought to ensure that this occurred. Such a rule of love would not only end tyranny but usher in the Kingdom of Christ. Man's 'actuall Religion', therefore, was 'to give an equall portion of worldly goods unto every man'. Perhaps not all radicals would agree with this last statement, but they would all agree that the rulers of England had hitherto been hypocrites who professed the Christian message while refusing to practise its essence, which was practical charity. Abiezer Coppe, in fiery language, told the rich to abase themselves before the poor if they wished to be considered true Christians. The social and political message of the radicals was built upon this foundation.

We have seen that in the 1640s Parliamentarian rhetoric shifted from that of royal counsellors to that of popular representatives and agents of God's work; we have seen how a rhetoric of moderation and peace was appealed to by both Royalists and Parliamentarians, but perhaps most successfully by the former. Parliament came in the end to require an activist rhetoric which made it increasingly difficult for it to appeal to traditional notions of order in ways that Royalists could. And, finally, we have seen how Parliament failed to keep control over its own activist rhetoric. The emergence in England of radicalism was, in part at least, the consequence of the fact that the conventional rhetorics of Godly Rule and popular representation available to Parliament were *too* activist. The appeal to God's will was certainly useful in justifying the actions of the late 1640s. But who could draw boundaries around what God might do or require? As Thomas Hobbes was to recognize in *Leviathan* (1651), if you make divine inspiration a sufficient justification of political activism, then you open the way for anyone to do as they wish since it is impossible to distinguish genuine from pretended inspiration.

But by 1651 England was a very different place. Perhaps the best indication of the importance of rhetoric in this decade is the fact that after the King's execution there was a rapid withdrawal from the activist rhetoric that had been employed in the 1640s. Defenders of the Rump employed themes that had been the staple of royalist propaganda in the 1640s. From 1649 onwards writers such as Anthony Ascham argued that peace and order required obedience to the new regime, even though it was illegal. Failure to give allegiance would only produce chaos, which would be in no one's interest. He also, like many Royalist predecessors, argued that most of the time private citizens had no business in judging their rulers: their lot was one of perpetual and willing subjection. As 1649 wore on, arguments such as these tended to replace those of the Commons' *Declaration* of 21 March. The year 1649 may have marked the victory of the army and the Independents in the Commons; but even more it marked the victory of rhetoric over theory. Those who won in 1649 were to spend a decade quietly replacing the arguments that helped to give them victory with the rhetoric of their enemies. It was only the fact that Oliver Cromwell was one of the few who were unwilling to do this that prevented their success.

Thomas Hobbes' Leviathan, *(1651) was the most important piece of political thinking of the period.*

CHAPTER V

The Impact of the New Model Army

IAN GENTLES

P arliament's war against the King had suffered a nearly disastrous loss of momentum by the autumn of 1644. Despite the stunning victory at Marston Moor the previous summer, the campaign in the south had virtually ground to a halt. Sir William Waller had been trounced at Roundway Down and Cropredy Bridge. The Earl of Essex, now seriously ill, had been humiliated at Lostwithiel. The army of the Eastern Association was rent by political and religious conflict, while its leader, the Earl of Manchester, had lost his appetite for victory.

In an effort to put an end to the recriminations that were crippling the Parliamentary effort, Zouch Tate, one of the most hawkish of Presbyterian MPs, introduced a motion to remove Members of both Houses of Parliament from all offices, military or civil, for the duration of the War. Although sponsored by Tate, the resolution was widely perceived as a radical ploy. The Earl of Essex's close allies in the Commons made a bid to exempt him from the provisions of the resolution. It was turned back by a narrow margin. Essex and Manchester then rallied their forces in the Lords to have the Self-Denying Ordinance thrown out.

Faced with the frustration of their plans, the hawks in the Commons now embarked on an outflanking manoeuvre against the majority in the Lords committed to a negotiated settlement. Over the next four months they set about the starvation of the existing armies of money, while creating a new army with new leaders, none of whom were Members of either House. Thus the Lords were finally browbeaten into accepting the new army by having the rug pulled from under their feet. The new army was to consist of 6,600 cavalry, 1,000 dragoons (mounted infantry) and 14,400 infantry, a total of 22,000 men, in addition to about 2,300 officers. It was to be financed by a monthly assessment of £53,000, which later rose to £60,000, and in 1649 to £120,000. In a sense the New Model did not represent a radical departure from past practice. It was basically an amalgamation of three existing armies, financed along similar lines, and for its first few months still under the authority of the Committee of Both Kingdoms, on which the ousted generals Essex and Manchester sat.

Sir Thomas Fairfax was named commander-in-chief. He had already chalked up an excellent military record in the north, untainted by the political in-fighting that had plagued the southern armies. Nevertheless, his appointment was a clear victory for the radicals against the supporters of the Earl of Essex. To signify their disgruntlement with the new army, Essex's followers in the Lords tried to alter a third of the officer list submitted by Fairfax for Parliament's approval. They demoted or excluded known radicals, and promoted or reintroduced

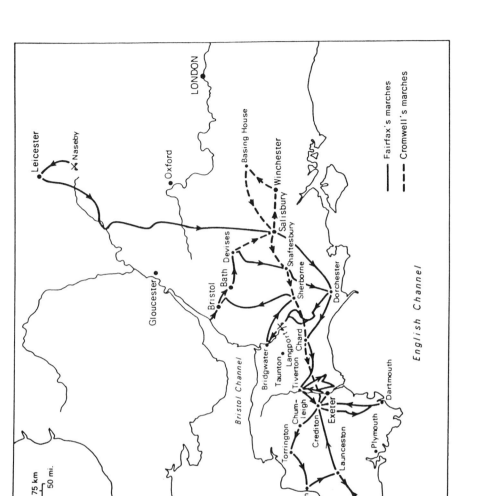

The campaign in the West, 1645-6.

Presbyterians and Scots who had been left off the list. Only after the Commons threatened to go ahead without them did the Lords finally approve Fairfax's list without changes, but then only by the narrowest margin.

The final passage of the Self-Denying Ordinance in April 1645, four months after its introduction in the House of Commons, signalled the collapse of aristocratic opposition to the new army. The Lords however would not swallow their hostility to Oliver Cromwell. When in June the Commons overrode the Ordinance by appointing him to the vacant lieutenant-generalship of the cavalry, the Lords balked. Only the stunning and unforeseen victory at Naseby a few days later made it impossible for them to continue blocking the appointment.

The sinews of war

A major reason for the New Model's success was that it was more generously financed than all of Parliament's other armies. Between its founding in April 1645 and June 1647 the foot were paid 76 per cent, and the cavalry 58 per cent of the time, which by seventeenth-century standards was a remarkable record. A second reason for the army's success was that it had unobstructed access to a great economic powerhouse – the metropolis of London. Vast quantities of

---

Glossary

AGITATORS: the representatives thrown up by the regiments during the spring of 1647. By June the companies and troops of most regiments had each elected two rank-and-file and two officer agitators. It was from this group that the General Council of the Army was drawn in July of the same year. In September and October new, more radical agitators (also known as agents) emerged in about a dozen regiments. At the time the term agitator did not have the negative connotation that it later acquired.

BAGGAGE TRAIN: the army's equipment, supplies and artillery, and the wagons used to transport them. Guarded by a unit of 200 firelocks or musketeers.

GRANDEES: the contemptuous label applied by Levellers and army radicals to the higher or staff officers, Cromwell and Ireton especially.

HALBERD: infantry weapon consisting of a sharp-edged blade ending in a point, and a spear-head, mounted on a handle five to seven feet long.

MAN OF BLOOD: the epithet consistently applied by the army to Charles I after the spring of 1648. The officers came to the collective conclusion that Charles, by conspiring with the Scots to unleash renewed Civil War in 1648, was singlehandedly responsible for all the bloodshed and suffering of that year. The defeat of his forces in every military engagement proved that he was also 'the man against whom God hath witnessed' and so vindicated the epithet. Guilty of high crimes against the English people, his inexorable fate must be to be tried for the innocent blood that had been spilt, and to expiate it with his life.

PIKE: infantry weapon consisting of a wooden shaft up to 16 feet long and a pointed iron head.

TRAINED BANDS: county or city militias. These part-time, partly-trained soldiers were inferior in fighting quality to the professional soldiers of the field army. The London trained bands for example, were almost as numerous as the New Model (18,000 against 22,000 men), but were no match for them during the crisis of 1647.

clothing, gunpowder, pikes, halberds, swords and muskets poured out of London workshops. For the other things the army required, it lived off the land. Except for an initial shipment of biscuit and Suffolk cheese, the soldiers bought their food locally out of their daily wage – eightpence for a foot soldier and two shillings for a cavalry trooper (who also had to feed his horse). The officers were paid several times more per day than the rank and file – thirty shillings for a colonel, £10 a day for the commander-in-chief. A soldier's normal diet consisted of hard biscuit, cheese and beer. Meat was a luxury. Fruit and root vegetables were regarded with contempt.

The year of victories, June 1645–June 1646
The new army got off to a shaky start. At the beginning of June the King caught the commanders off guard when he swooped down on Leicester and brutally sacked it. Puffed up by this triumph, he allowed his advisers to persuade him that he would have no trouble crushing the entire 'New Noddle' as they scornfully nicknamed it. So he committed his greatest blunder of the war by attacking a force almost twice as large as his own at Naseby in Northamptonshire. For all Fairfax's numerical superiority the battle was in fact a close call. Prince Rupert, commanding the right wing of the Royalist cavalry, steamrollered the Parliamentary left wing under the less experienced Commissary-General Henry Ireton. The Parliamentary infantry did not stand up well under the first Royalist charge, and was in danger of collapse after its commander, Major-General Philip Skippon, was severely wounded and had to leave the field. Only a determined effort by Fairfax and Cromwell saved the day. Cromwell, assisted by Colonel Okey and his crack regiment of dragoons, rescued the left wing from total defeat, while Fairfax reformed the entire army for a second advance. On the right wing Cromwell led a successful charge against Langdale and drove the King's cavalry off the field. Rupert, who had allowed his men to ride off in pursuit of the New Model's baggage train, returned to the battlefield too late to affect the outcome. It was a tremendous victory for the untried army. Losing only 150 men, the New Model killed 1,000 of the King's infantry and took 4,000 prisoners.

Apart from a few anxious moments, the rest of the first Civil War was essentially a mopping-up campaign. In July at Langport the only other Royalist cavalry force in the field was destroyed. Fortresses that dared to hold out against their besiegers soon tumbled at the shuddering impact of New Model artillery (Bridgwater, Sherborne, Berkeley Castle, Devizes, Basing and Tiverton), or from the furious assault of the infantry (Bath and Bristol).

In June 1646, with only his Oxford headquarters intact, Charles fled to Newark where he surrendered to the Scots. Oxford fell a few days later and the year of wonders was over. The army was now about to embark upon the treacherous seas of political intrigue. What lay ahead was a much more subtle and complicated war of political manoeuvre that would be fought with petitions, pamphlets and secret plots. The army's radicalization was to begin in the near future.

The importance of religion
Before examining that chapter in the New Model's history, we need first to understand the shaping influence of religion on the army's character, and how

it in turn affected English society. The New Model is unique among modern armies, not only in its religious observances, but in the frequency with which it resorted to theological arguments in its public pronouncements. This is not to say that the whole army was imbued with religious fervour. A high proportion of the infantry were conscripted, and from them there was a constant stream of deserters. Other infantry were Royalist prisoners of war who simply switched sides in order to continue their military career. Furthermore there are continual reports of a scoffing attitude towards religion among some of the officers and the rank and file.

Having said this, it remains true that four of the five generals – Fairfax, Cromwell, Skippon and Ireton (Thomas Hammond being the possible exception) – were devout Puritans. So were a high proportion of the lower-ranking officers. These men stamped the army with the imprint of their own piety and zeal. They shared a conviction that they were the instruments of divine providence, frequently expressing a thirst for the destruction of Antichrist and the coming of the millennium. This fervour is also found among many of the rank and file. The chaplain William Dell testified that he had sometimes accidentally overheard troopers praying '. . . with that faith and familiarity with God that [I] have stood wondering at the grace'. Captain Hodgson, while riding in darkness past his own lines on the eve of the Battle of Dunbar, heard a cornet praying aloud, 'exceedingly carried on in the duty. I met with so much of God in it, as I was satisfied deliverance was at hand'. This habit of vocal, extemporaneous prayer won for the New Model the reputation of 'the praying army'.

Religious zeal was fortified at every opportunity. The chaplains delivered frequent sermons, which drew large, attentive crowds. Bible study was pursued in many units. The officers habitually called days of fasting and humiliation to seek God's blessing and to prepare the army spiritually for battle. Iconography reinforced the providential consciousness – mottoes on standards, like 'pray and fight' (Skippon); 'for the protestants' (Graves), 'With God as our guide, there is no need to despair' (Sheffield); and passwords in battle: 'God our strength' at Naseby, 'God with us' at Dartmouth, 'Emmanuel' at Torrington, and 'the Lord of Hosts' at Dunbar and Worcester. Fasts, prayers and days of humiliation were also used during times of political crisis. One jaundiced observer was convinced that all the officers' political mischief was 'ever done after fasting and prayer'.

Intense piety was often accompanied by exaggerated humility and self-abasement. Curiously, the more powerful the army grew the more it insisted on its weakness and humility. At Naseby Oliver Cromwell said that God had given the victory to 'a company of poor ignorant men'. Officers frequently repudiated any reliance on 'the arm of flesh', professing to depend on God's help alone. No doubt they felt flattered and reassured when the preacher John Maudit told them in 1649 that God chooses 'the poor contemptible ones of the world that are rich in faith . . . to bring his great designs about'.

Many soldiers were also zealous evangelists of God's word. In defiance of a Parliamentary ban on lay preaching, officers not only preached to their own men, but elbowed incumbent ministers out of their pulpits up and down England. Marshall-General Richard Laurence vindicated these activities with the observation that the country people were in desperate need of having the gospel preached to them.

Hugh Peter, fiery army preacher, Leveller sympathizer and supporter of the regicide.

The godliness that was so actively promoted in the army fostered high morale and an exacting standard of personal conduct. Many commented on the sense of unity and fellowship that they encountered among all ranks. This partly arose out of the harsh code of discipline imposed by Sir Thomas Fairfax at the very beginning of the army's career. Behaviour that is regarded with indulgence in most armies – swearing, drunkenness and fornication – was frowned upon in the New Model. Notorious blasphemers were bored through the tongue with a hot iron; drunkards were forced to ride the wooden horse – a painful as well as humiliating punishment; sexual transgressors were whipped and cashiered. But Puritan discipline had a positive side too. The preaching of Peter, Dell and Saltmarsh promoted egalitarianism. A striking example of the fruits of egalitarianism was the establishment of the General Council of the Army in 1647, when each regiment elected representatives to deliberate on army affairs and debate England's constitutional future.

The other side of the coin of fellowship and equality was a sense of alienation and separation from the rest of society. The officers admonished one another not to walk in the ways of the world, because they were 'strangers and pilgrims here travelling . . . towards our own country and city, whose maker and builder is God'. They could thus rationalize the fact that most people were against them. The hostile majority were dismissed as a corrupt and ungodly mass who 'support the Beast and oppose the advancement of the kingdom of our Lord Jesus Christ'.

The army's religious fervour had practical results. The conviction that they were fighting the warfare of heaven bred in them the courage to perform acts of daring and improvisation both on the battlefield and in the political arena. By the autumn of 1648, stiffened by inflammatory preaching and scriptural texts, they took aim at Charles I, 'that man of blood', the 'man against whom God hath witnessed'. Propelled by this conviction, they rode roughshod over the will of the people, to bring the King to his public trial and execution.

Later, people would feel the force of the New Model's religious zeal in the keenness with which it attempted to enforce the Puritan reformation of manners – the suppression of stage plays, of cruel sports like bear-baiting and cock fighting, of holidays like Christmas and Ascension Day, and of alehouses. It was tireless in its enforcement of the Sabbath. More important in the army's mind however, was its role as a protector of the godly against their ungodly persecutors. Many Independent and sectarian congregations were only too conscious that the army was a prop to their survival. In London, Bristol, Hull and numerous smaller towns, the army was 'a shelter to honest people that had otherwise been hammered to dust'.

In sum, the religious energy with which the army was so copiously endowed, had an impact both on the battlefield and upon civilian society. Few of the activities just described were those of a normal army; they are directly traceable to the New Model's peculiar religious stamp.

The army and the people

The army's religious zeal was but one source of friction with many civilians. During the hiatus between the first and second Civil Wars, those who had welcomed the glittering parade of victories against the King began to wonder why it was still necessary to keep up an expensive, idle military machine. It became harder to collect the monthly assessment, and this interrupted the regularity of army pay. As a result the soldiers were impelled increasingly to rely on free quarter. If the householders on whom they were lodged did not furnish the food they needed the soldiers were more than ready to fend for themselves, confiscating grain and hay, rounding up and slaughtering livestock, and poaching game. If horses were needed, the soldiers simply seized them. In 1646 soldiers were also assigned the unpopular task of collecting the monthly assessment. One economic result of this military predation was that many tenants could not pay their rents. Landlords' revenues shrank by as much as a third.

Idle soldiers were also prone to become sexual predators. The army left, as William Prynne angrily put it, 'not a few great bellies and bastards on the inhabitants' and countries' charge'.

More and more the soldiers came to be seen as parasites. Friction often flared into violence, which then left a legacy of implacable hostility between soldiers and civilians. To protect themselves from civilian antagonism the soldiers got Parliament to pass an ordinance in June 1647 guaranteeing indemnity for all acts committed while in arms for the service of Parliament. The commissioners empowered under the ordinance dealt with over 1,100 military cases, indicating that considerably more than that number of soldiers had been subject to judicial prosecution for acts committed while in uniform.

By far the commonest grievance against the soldiers was the seizure of horses. Next came complaints about the seizure of goods, provisions, livestock and weapons, followed by disputes over quarters, money, debts and arrears. Thus, while most of the conflict recorded in the Indemnity Papers arose out of material issues, it is surprising how much of the antipathy towards the soldiers had to do with ideology. Through the medium of these documents we hear soldiers being denounced as 'Roundhead rogues', 'Parliament dogs' and 'Parliament whores'. Time and again we hear people venting their rage against an army which is about to topple the monarchy or has just done so. In every part of the country we witness the animosity aroused by the soldiers on account of their Puritan evangelization and their destruction of the visible symbols of popery and prelacy.

Presbyterians and Independents (as Political 'Parties')

By 1645 the two major political groupings in the House of Commons had acquired religious labels. The Presbyterians were followers of the Earl of Essex. Conservative in social and political matters, and opposed to religious toleration, they favoured a negotiated peace with the King. Between 1645 and 1647 they became progressively disenchanted with the New Model Army, and drew closer to the Scots. Their support for a Presbyterian Church settlement derived mainly from their conviction that it would act as a bulwark against social revolution. The Independents believed in the vigorous prosecution of the war against the King. Unhappy with the authoritarianism of Scottish Presbyterianism, they favoured a more loosely structured national Church that would allow a considerable measure of liberty of conscience. They were enthusiastic about the creation of the New Model Army, and defended it against Presbyterian efforts to disband it in 1647. They were also sympathetic to radical proposals for the abolition of tithes, the broadening of the franchise and the dismantling of the monopolies of the great London trading companies. Neither party commanded the consistent allegiance of more than a few dozen Members of the Commons. There was in addition a small Middle Group, but most MPs were aligned to no political faction. (See information box on p.62.)

The political wars, 1647–48

The army's unpopularity played into the hands of Essex's party, now acquiring the label Presbyterian. In February 1647 they persuaded Parliament to reduce the army to just over a quarter of its strength in England, and to send most of the infantry to Ireland. The New Model's defenders seemed powerless to prevent its virtual disbandment. In London the radical Independents – soon to be known as Levellers – exhorted Parliament in their 'Large Petition' not to 'lay by that strength which (under God) hath hitherto made you powerful . . .' At about the same time the rank and file started petitioning for indemnity, arrears of pay, an end to conscription, and compensation to maimed soldiers and the families of the slain. When Fairfax failed to suppress this petitioning activity Holles prevailed upon the Commons to pass the 'Declaration of Dislike' which defined soldiers who continued petitioning as 'enemies of the state'. The Declaration opened an unbreachable chasm of distrust between the Presbyterian leadership and the army. It was the perceived attempt by Parliament to divide and destroy them that transformed the soldiers' mood into one of revolutionary militancy. Their first demand now became the vindication of their honour by the expunging of the 'Declaration of Dislike'.

In the spring of 1647 it was the rank and file who spearheaded the army's militancy. Their resolution inspired most of the officers to stick with them during the confrontation with Parliament. In the end a quarter of the officers remained loyal to Parliament, which meant that they had to quit the army or were driven out. The political militants were known as agitators. By early May most regiments had chosen up to two of these representatives from each troop and company to act on their behalf. They became the foundation of a unique if short-lived experiment in military democracy.

Under the impetus of the agitators the army drew together for a collective rendezvous near Newmarket on 5 June. In the meantime Cornet George Joyce and 500 cavalry, with the blessing of Oliver Cromwell, had wrested the King from his Presbyterian guards at Holdenby. Joyce exceeded his instructions however, by spiriting Charles away to army headquarters. The grandees now decided that it was high time they reasserted control over the army. Probably under Ireton's inspiration they moved for the creation of an army council, consisting of two officers and two rankers from each regiment, plus the fifteen or so officers of the general staff. The Newmarket rendezvous was an intoxicating experience of unity, climaxed by the unanimous adoption of a Solemn Engagement not to permit themselves to be divided or disbanded until all the army's grievances had been redressed.

Over the summer and autumn of 1647 agitators and grandees worked in close collaboration. We know that the agitators' activities were approved of, if not directed by the general staff, since records show that their travel expenses, printing bills and various perquisites, were all paid for out of the army's contingency fund. Even the arrest of Colonel Sedenham Poynts, the Presbyterian colonel-general of the Northern Army, was financed by army headquarters. During July the agitators pressed for a march on London to expel the Presbyterian ringleaders from Parliament, restore the London militia to friendly hands (the Presbyterians had had it purged of Independents), and free John Lilburne and other radicals from prison.

Chronology

9 DECEMBER 1644 Self-Denying Resolution excluding Members of both Houses of Parliament from all offices, military and civil, for the duration of the war, is introduced into the Commons by Zouch Tate.

15 FEBRUARY 1645 Ordinance creating the New Model Army is passed.

14 JUNE 1645 The New Model defeats the King's forces at Naseby.

24 JUNE 1646 First Civil War ends with the surrender of Royalist headquarters at Oxford.

18 FEBRUARY 1647 House of Commons resolution to disband most of the New Model, and ship several regiments to Ireland.

2 JUNE 1647 Cornet George Joyce seizes the King at Holdenby, Northamptonshire and removes him to Newmarket.

5 JUNE 1647 At a rendezvous near Newmarket the New Model adopts a Solemn Engagement not to disband until all grievances are redressed. The General Council of the Army is established, comprising four representatives from each regiment and the general staff.

26 JULY 1647 A counter-revolutionary crowd assaults Parliament; Independent MPs flee to the army.

2 AUGUST 1647 Having failed to win the King's support for it, the army publishes its programme for the settlement of the kingdom, known as the Heads of the Proposals.

6 AUGUST 1647 The army occupies Westminster and escorts Independent MPs to Whitehall.

28 OCTOBER 1647 The General Council of the Army assembles at Putney to begin debating *The Case of the Armie Truly Stated* and the Agreement of the People.

15 NOVEMBER 1647 The first of three army rendezvous is held at Corkbush Field near Ware, Hertfordshire (the other two are held a few days later near Watford and Kingston). A Leveller-inspired mutiny is suppressed.

JANUARY–APRIL 1648 Disbandment reduces the combined New Model and garrison forces from 44,000 to 24,000.

29 OCTOBER 1648 Colonel Thomas Rainborowe, the highest-ranking Leveller supporter in the army, is killed by Royalists at Doncaster.

20 NOVEMBER 1648 The Remonstrance of the Army is laid before Parliament.

2 DECEMBER 1648 The army occupies Westminster.

6 DECEMBER 1648 Pride's Purge.

20–27 JANUARY 1649 The High Court established by Parliament tries and condemns Charles I for treason.

30 JANUARY 1649 Execution of Charles I.

14–15 MAY 1649 Suppression of the Leveller-inspired mutiny at Burford.

Partly to forestall the agitators' demand for a march on London, Ireton and the higher officers introduced the Heads of the Proposals, which they had formulated in consultation with the faction of radical peers led by Lords Saye and Wharton. Radical and far-reaching, the Proposals were also the most generous constitutional package Charles was ever offered. The electoral map was to be redrawn, while tithes, trade monopolies, the excise and imprisonment for debt were abolished. On the other hand people would be permitted to use the Book of Common Prayer, and the episcopate would continue, though with bishops stripped of their coercive power. Parliament was to control the armed forces for ten years, not twenty as the Newcastle Propositions had demanded, while judges and other high officers of state would be appointed by Parliament for ten years only, not in perpetuity.

Talks with the King were overtaken by events in London. On 22 July the Commons, continuing its appeasement of the army, returned the London militia to Independent hands. This provoked despairing Presbyterian extremists in the capital to attempt a counter-revolutionary coup. An angry mob besieged Parliament demanding reinstatement of the Presbyterian-dominated militia committee, and the King's presence in London without prior conditions. Lords and Commons both capitulated before the violent crowd, but the Independent minority in each House fled to the army for protection.

The actions of the Presbyterian mob vindicated the militants' call for a march on London. With the help of the Southwark Trained Bands, the New Model occupied the capital without firing a shot, and escorted its Parliamentary supporters back to their seats in Westminster. Independents resumed control over the London militia committee, while their Parliamentary enemies fled, and the mayor with several Presbyterian aldermen were confined to the Tower. On Saturday 7 August the army staged a calculated show of force by marching slowly through the streets of the City. To the dismay of the Presbyterian magistrates, the soldiers were applauded by many of the common people as they passed by.

With the army on their doorstep, the Levellers now strove to infiltrate it and dominate its political agenda. One fruit of their efforts was the emergence of new, more radical agitators, or agents, in a dozen regiments. In October the agents from five cavalry regiments put their names to The Case of the Armie Truly Stated – a massive indictment of the senior officers for their political moderation, and a clarion call for complete religious freedom, the abolition of conscription, and votes for all freeborn Englishmen except Royalists. Their fundamental axiom was that 'all power is originally and essentially in the whole body of the people of this nation'. Hence the Long Parliament was to be speedily dissolved, with elections every two years, based on equal constituencies. The oppression of the people would be lifted by doing away with monopolies, tithes, and the excise tax on beer, cloth and other English commodities.

In striving to forge an alliance between the common people and the army the Levellers faced an almost insurmountable obstacle. The people craved relief from taxation, while the army depended on heavy taxation – the monthly assessment – for its very existence. Nevertheless, as Cromwell admitted, the Levellers had made deep inroads into the army, and it was this fact which obligated the General Council to debate the new agents' demands at Putney, a London suburb, at the end of October 1647. Bolstered by their civilian friends

35

those people, That by the Civill Constitution of this ___
Kingedome, which is originall and fundamentall, and ___
beyond which I am sure noe Memory of Record doth goe
(not before the Conquest) but before the Conquest itt was
soe, Yf itt bee intended that those that by that Constitution
that was before the Conquest that hath bin beyond memory
such psons that have bin before that Constitution should bee
the Electors I have noe more to say agt. itt.

Col: Rainborow. Moved, That others might have given their hands ___ to itt.

Capt. Denne, Denied, That those that were sent of their Regimt that they were their Hands.

Comiss. Ireton, Whether those Men whose hands are to itt, or those that ___ brought itt doe knowe soe much of this Matter as that they ___ meane that all that had a former Right of Election, or those that had noe right before are to come in?

Co: Cowling. In the time before the Conquest, and since the Conquest ___ the greatest pte of the Kingdome was in vassalage.

cnt. Pettus. Wee judge, That all Inhabitants that have nott lost their Birthright should have an equall voice in Elections.

Col: Rainborow. I desired that those that had engaged in itt for really I thinke that the poorest hee that is in England hath a life to live as the greatest hee, and therefore (Truly Sr) I thinke itts cleare that every Man that is to live under a Government ought first by his owne Consent to put himself under that Government, and

*T*he text of the Putney Debates of 1647
were taken down in shorthand by William Clarke,
and then transcribed as here.

95

John Wildman and Maximilian Petty, the new agents tabled a document entitled The Agreement of the People. It contained two novel concepts: the circulation of a written constitution which people would ratify by affixing their signatures; and powers that would be reserved for the people alone, not to be exercised by any government.

Cromwell, alarmed at the 'very great alterations' this implied, questioned whether the people of England would actually support the Agreement. The Levellers found an unexpected ally in Colonel Thomas Rainborowe who was untroubled by the document's revolutionary implications and entered the fray with the assertion that 'there hath been many scufflings between the honest men of England and those that have tyrannized over them'.

Commissary-General Henry Ireton attacked the Agreement for its implied advocacy of universal manhood suffrage, which he was sure would lead to the destruction of property. Rainborowe took up this challenge in words of ringing eloquence:

> Really I think that the poorest he that is in England hath a life to live as the greatest he; and therefore truly, sir, I think it's clear, that every man that is to live under a government ought first by his own consent to put himself under that government.

Few in the General Council supported Ireton except Cromwell and Colonels Rich and Waller (Fairfax was ill at the time). Perceiving that the Levellers were running away with the argument, Cromwell took the bull by the horns, cut off debate and sent the agitators back to their regiments. He and the grandees were able to do this because they had already acquiesced in another general rendezvous of the army, and were also known to be vigorously pressing the army's material demands.

For both practical and political reasons the senior officers decided to divide the regiments into three separate rendezvous. Several of the most radical ones however, were not invited. Four of them disobeyed orders and marched to the first rendezvous at Corkbush Field near Ware in Hertfordshire. Most notable was Colonel Robert Lilburne's regiment, which defied orders to march to Newcastle. Two men were killed and an officer wounded in the fray before they got to Ware. At the rendezvous itself Thomas Rainborowe, no longer technically a member of the army (having recently been appointed vice-admiral of the navy), tried to present a petition to Fairfax urging adoption of the Agreement of the People. The men of Thomas Harrison's horse regiment appeared without their officers, wearing copies of the Agreement pinned to their hats. Fairfax brushed aside these challenges to his authority and read out a Remonstrance to Parliament which satisfied most soldiers. But the day's turbulent events were not over. When Major Gregson attempted to restore order to Colonel Lilburne's regiment he was met with a hail of stones and suffered a broken head. Furious, Cromwell and some other officers stormed through the mutinous ranks, swords drawn, tearing the Agreement from the soldiers' hats with their own hands.

Once the officers had re-established order they bent their efforts to conciliating the alienated radicals, and exerted greater pressure on Parliament to redress material grievances. Unity was patched up, while constant pay was resumed for the next several months. On its side, Parliament insisted that the people's

*S*ir *Thomas Fairfax presiding over the Council of the Army, 1647.*

burdens be eased by reducing the land forces in England from about 44,000 to 24,000. The great disbandment was carried through in January and February 1648, but the army's general staff saw to it that most of the original New Model regiments were preserved intact.

The second Civil War

Even as the last few thousand men were being demobilized, Royalist insurrection was erupting in the capital, and disturbing reports were reaching headquarters of imminent armed rebellion in the Western border counties, Wales, the North, East Anglia, Kent and Essex. The war, which was more a series of poorly co-ordinated uprisings against Parliamentary oppression, was triggered by Charles's success at concluding an engagement with the Scots at the end of 1647. Having entrusted London to the reliable care of Major-General Philip Skippon, the officers then set about ruthlessly snuffing out Royalist brushfires in the southern half of the country and in Wales. After this was accomplished they turned to meet the combined Scottish and Royalist forces in the North. The devastating defeat inflicted upon them near Preston in August left Parliament free to impose whatever terms it wished upon Charles I.

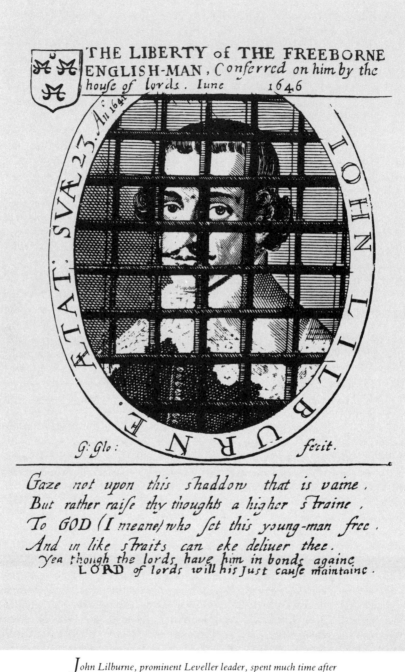

*J*ohn Lilburne, prominent Leveller leader, spent much time after
1645 and wrote most of his tracts, while imprisoned by the
Parliament.

But to the officers' astonishment, Parliament launched a round of leisurely negotiations at Newport, lending a sympathetic ear to the King's demands. Army thinking had been moving in a contrary direction for more than half a year. In April, distress at the renewed outbreak of Civil War had led the officers to a three-day marathon of fasting and prayer. Its culmination was an emotional catharsis, expressed in the floods of tears that poured from the eyes of every participant. Without dissent they agreed that after they had crushed their enemies they would 'call for Charles Stuart, that man of blood, to an account for that blood he had shed, and mischief he had done . . . against the Lord's cause and people in these poor nations . . .'

Thus in the autumn of 1648 it was a far more radical body of men who pondered their strategy, than the group which had trembled before defying Parliament the previous year. Even the conservative Henry Ireton was now receptive to an alliance with the Levellers whom he had originally scorned.

The political crisis was exacerbated by the killing of Thomas Rainborowe. The radical colonel's death at the hands of Royalist agents in Doncaster was interpreted in the army as the deliberate murder of one of the people's most effective advocates. His funeral turned into a political protest by London Levellers and their army friends.

In this charged atmosphere Fairfax summoned the Council of Officers to a series of meetings, beginning on 7 November. Over the course of these meetings the Remonstrance drafted by Henry Ireton was approved for presentation to Parliament. Its key demand was that Parliament, as the sovereign power, should have the sole right to define the public interest and call offenders to account, even if they had broken no existing law. The revolutionary quality of the Remonstrance was its indictment of Charles for breaking his covenant to protect the people's rights and liberties. Since he was guilty of all the innocent blood shed in the recent Civil War, God's wrath against the nation could only be appeased by executing judgment against him.

John Lilburne, who was well briefed on the content of the Remonstrance, was dismayed at the prospect of the army taking the law into its own hands. While he could not deflect the officers from their determination to try the King, he was successful in having an endorsement of the Leveller programme inserted into the Remonstrance. The officers went so far as to urge Parliament to adopt the Agreement of the People as England's constitution. They also agreed to Lilburne's proposal for a sixteen-man committee representing four parties – the Levellers, the army, London Independents and the 'honest party' in Parliament – to explore how these goals were to be realized.

In the immediate context Lilburne's gains were of no consequence, for on 20 November the Commons laid aside the Remonstrance and returned to their peace negotiations with the King. Appreciating that a peace treaty between Charles and Parliament spelt their own extinction as an organized force, the officers now crossed their political Rubicon. On 2 December they marched 7,000 troops into Westminster, intending thereby to intimidate the Commons into purging themselves of 'corrupt and apostasized members'. But when, after an all-night sitting the MPs, with reckless courage, voted that the King's answer to their propositions at Newport was an acceptable basis for continued negotiations, the officers decided to do the purging themselves. On

---

The Agreement of the People

The Levellers' draft constitution for England. It was published in four versions: (1) The First Agreement, 3 November 1647, which was debated by the General Council of the Army at Putney; (2) The Second Agreement, December 1648, drafted by the 16-man committee representing Levellers, the army, London Independents and the 'honest party' in Parliament, and submitted to the Council of Officers who debated it at Whitehall during the weeks before the King's execution. As amended by them it became known as (3) The Officers' Agreement, submitted to the House of Commons on 20 January 1649. (4) The Third Agreement was published by the imprisoned Leveller leaders on 1 May 1649 in an attempt to rally popular support against the grandees.

All versions of the agreement provided for the dissolution of the Long Parliament, electoral redistribution according to population, biennial Parliaments, and the undivided sovereignty of a single-chamber Parliament. The Agreement also contained the novel concept of reserved powers, in other words powers which no Parliament could exercise, since they were reserved by the people to themselves. They included the power to compel religious belief, the power of conscription, and the power to sanction any departure from the principle of equality before the law.

The Levellers intended that the Agreement should be circulated among the adult males of England. No one who refused to sign it would have the right to vote or participate in political affairs. The Officers' Agreement eliminated this requirement, calling simply for the enactment of the document by Parliamentary ordinance.

It should be noted that the Agreement, both in the December version endorsed by the Levellers, and in the officers' version of January 1649,

---

the morning of 6 December the men of Pride's and Rich's regiments filled the streets adjacent to the House of Commons. Assisted by Lord Grey of Groby, Colonel Pride arrested 41 of the MPs on his list of 80 or 90 that the officers had drawn up the day before. The officers then sent a message to the House demanding that it execute justice, dissolve itself, and then 'provide for a speedy succession of equal Representatives according to our late Remonstrance'.

Oliver Cromwell arrived in London from the North the day after Pride's Purge. Throughout the autumn he had made clear his support for the alliance with the Levellers, the Remonstrance of the Army, the purging or dissolving of Parliament, and the trial of the King. But for the next several weeks he cultivated Parliamentary moderates, obtaining the release of some of the imprisoned MPs, and showing himself solicitous of the views of middle-of-the-roaders like Bulstrode Whitelocke and Sir Thomas Widdrington. This conciliatory work was designed to win as many MPs as possible to the revolutionary cause. At all times Cromwell was at one with his fellow-officers in their resolve to bring the King to justice.

would have sharply limited the franchise. At the time it was freely conceded that the excluded groups – active Royalists, servants and wage-earners – comprised over half the potential male electorate. Candidates for election were to be subjected to even more stringent qualifications. Barred from the first two Representatives were any who had aided the King, signed the London Engagement calling for a personal treaty with the King in the summer of 1647, petitioned for a truce with the Scots invaders, or offered any compliance with the rebels in the second Civil War. When such limitations were imposed in the London municipal elections of December 1648 the result was a revolutionary takeover of the Common Council. Thus, for the short term the Agreement would have prepared the way, not so much for a democratic state as something resembling a dictatorship of the 'godly' or at least the 'well-affected'.

On Ireton's insistence the Officer's Agreement stipulated that Christianity was to be the state religion, and provided for a tolerant Established Church. Other changes sought by Ireton were thwarted however, and the final version that was submitted to Parliament on behalf of the army was essentially a victory for the lower officers.

But for the Levellers, the document was fatally flawed, not only by its selling out of the principle of religious toleration, but also by being submitted for approval to Parliament instead of to the English people. Accordingly, after their final breach with the grandees, the Levellers issued the Third (and most radical) Agreement on 1 May 1649. The requirement that men sign in order to benefit from it was silently dropped, as was the elaborate list of activities which would disqualify one from the franchise. Only servants, almstakers and those who had actively assisted the late King would be barred. By the spring of 1649 Leveller hatred of the grandees had become so all-consuming that they did not much care if the Royalists got back into power.

Meanwhile John Lilburne's Committee of Sixteen had been deliberating. A week after Pride's Purge it tendered a revised version of the Agreement of the People to the Council of Officers. Most of its content was accepted by the officers without dissent. But thanks to Henry Ireton there was a lengthy debate on freedom of conscience. His stubbornness resulted in a new provision for a loosely-structured Established Church. The lower officers however, combined to defeat Ireton on a number of other issues.

When the officers laid their version of the Agreement before the Commons on 20 January the MPs murmured a few polite words but then did nothing. Nor did the army exert any further active pressure to implement the Agreement of the People. This was less likely because the higher officers regarded the document as a 'children's rattle' with which to distract the Levellers from the King's trial, than because their ardour for the Agreement had been cooled by the Levellers' very success against Ireton in the Council of Officers.

Indeed, the Levellers' greatest blunder was to try and stir up the rank and file to wrest power from their officers with the accusation that they had watered down the Agreement and betrayed the Newmarket Engagement. By their vitriolic attacks on the grandees in the late winter of 1649 the Levellers lost most of their friends in Parliament and the officer corps. Whereas the overwhelming majority of army officers had backed the Levellers during the Whitehall debates, the Leveller-inspired mutiny culminating at Burford in May 1649, was supported by no commissioned officers except Major Cobbett and Cornet Denne.

While the Whitehall debates were proceeding, and moderates were being conciliated, the army tightened its grip on the King. The purged House of Commons read an indictment of Charles broadly similar to the one promulgated by the soldiers a few days before. It then set up a High Court of Justice to try him for treason against his own kingdom. 29 of the court's 135 commissioners were serving officers, but several were irregular in their attendance and refused to sign the death warrant. Most notorious of the abstainers was the commander-in-chief, Sir Thomas Fairfax who, as his wife put it, had more wit than to be there.

The business of the court was driven on by a knot of army grandees and revolutionary MPs. They collaborated to cast off the authority of the House of Lords, neutralize disaffected MPs, silence the protesting Presbyterian clergy of London, sidetrack Leveller discontent with a vote of £3,000 to John Lilburne, and stall the foreign ambassadors endeavouring to save the King's life. The Royalists, immobilized by shock and disbelief at the unfolding tragedy, did not present a problem.

In spite of a few embarrassing moments and the impressive eloquence of Charles in his own defence, it did not take the Court long to find him guilty. In the end the signatories to the death warrant numbered only 57, a figure which would have been lower had Cromwell not stood at the door of the House of Commons calling on his fellow MPs to add their names. 18 of the signatories were officers in active service, while a further seven had served previously. As the denouement approached, the officers' unity fractured. Not only did several avoid signing the death warrant – men like Skippon, Lambert, Fleetwood and Disbrowe – but on the morning of the execution there was an unseemly quarrel over who would sign the order for it to be carried out. When on that cold windy 30 January afternoon beneath a leaden sky Charles stepped onto the scaffold outside his Banqueting House in Whitehall, there were virtually no higher officers present to witness the scene. The moment the executioner's axe severed his head from his body the packed crowd gave out a deep groan, expressive of their horror at the unprecedented act of regicide.

Even while the event was being played out, the new rulers of England were moving swiftly to consolidate their power. Monarchy and House of Lords were abolished, as well as the chief executive body of the previous two years, the Derby House Committee. In its place a Council of State was instituted. Fully a third of the men named by the Commons to the Council had military connections, including generals Fairfax, Cromwell and Skippon. But the exclusion of the army's chief theoretician, Henry Ireton, and its most prominent millenarian, Thomas Harrison, was a stinging rebuke to these men's political ambitions. Equally, it was an unmistakable message that the Rump Parliament had no intention of letting England be ruled by a military dictatorship.

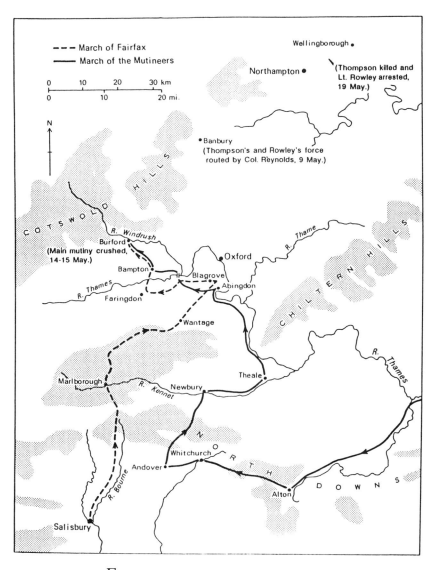

- - - March of Fairfax
—— March of the Mutineers

Wellingborough •

Northampton •

(Thompson killed and
Lt. Rowley arrested,
19 May.)

• Banbury
(Thompson's and Rowley's force
routed by Col. Reynolds, 9 May.)

COTSWOLD HILLS

R. Windrush
Burford •
(Main mutiny crushed,
14-15 May.)

Bampton •

• Oxford

R. Thame

CHILTERN HILLS

Blagrove
Abingdon

R. Thames
Faringdon •

Wantage •

Marlborough •

R. Kennet
Newbury

Theale •

R. Thames

NORTH

Whitchurch
Andover •

DOWNS

Alton •

R. Bourne

Salisbury •

*F*airfax and Cromwell's pursuit of the mutineers to Burford.

103

CHAPTER VI

The Impact on Society: A World Turned Upside Down?

JOHN WALTER

For many contemporaries, the social impact of the 1640s could be captured in the image of the world turned upside down. The decade began with elections to Parliament in which, it was complained, 'fellows without shirts challenge as good a voice as [gentlemen]'. As the decade progressed, Parliament's destruction of the structures of Charles I's authoritarian government was paralleled by popular destruction of enclosures and challenges to the authority of the landed classes, its destruction of Laudianism by the defacing of churches by people and troops. Parliament's claims for greater powers for itself were accompanied by popular demands for greater spiritual and political liberties, to which the collapse of royal and episcopal authority gave louder voice. The collapse of censorship allowed an unprecedented discussion in public and in print (many thousands of cheap pamphlets were produced in the period) which questioned the social, as well as the political and religious, order. Most alarmingly, the decade which had begun with demands for the restoration of the 'ancient constitution and fundamental law', had ended in political revolution with the fall of the monarchy and the rise of radical groups demanding a new constitution and a radical extension of rights for the people.

Contemporaries were ready to believe in the imminence of social inversion for three reasons: their experience of the destabilizing impact of longer-term social and economic trends on their society, their knowledge of the close correspondence between hierarchy in the state and in society, and the image of the people as the many-headed monster.

In the century before 1640 the population of the country had almost doubled. Directly, population growth had led to land shortage and landlessness, a trend exacerbated by the engrossing of land by landlords and richer farmers. Indirectly, the failure of agriculture to keep food supply in step with population led to inflation and a decline in wages. These changes brought a greater dependence on the market for both food and work for anything between a third and a half of the population and created greater instability in an economy where harvest failure led to unemployment, savagely spiralling food prices and, in some regions, even famine. As magistrates or MPs, gentlemen had had to grapple with the problems these changes created: food shortage, poor relief, rising levels of (reported) crime and, more worryingly, food and enclosure riots. The most visible symptom of these changes was the growth in the vagrant poor, who combined high visibility with alarming anonymity, masterless men and women without a place in settled society and therefore, master or minister to govern them. (In reality, as will be argued later, the outcome of these changes had also enlarged the scope for order.)

Tutored by the policies of the state and the preachings of the Church, many gentlemen regarded the people as fickle and irrational, the many-headed monster. This view of the people mingled fear as well as contempt. History, as well as their readings about the plebs in the ancient world prescribed by their classical education, warned them that the people were capable of challenging their rule. In the early 1640s there was a paper war in which in speech and pamphlet gentlemen referred to this earlier history of disorder to discourage each other from taking up arms. Naturally, this was a theme to which the King and his supporters gave constant refrain.

No King, no bishop; no bishop, no gentleman encapsulated the belief in the mutual relationship between political, religious and social hierarchies. That the first two were toppled, and the props of law, religion and even the family questioned in the 1640s, threatened the third. In the 1640s, religion, 'the legitimizing ideology of the rulers' threatened to become 'the revolutionary idiom of the ruled'.

It is important to recognize therefore that it was both against their experience of longer-term stresses and strains, as well as their own beliefs about the character and intentions of the people – increasingly orchestrated by a cacophony of references to Jack Straw and Wat Tyler (leaders of the rising of 1381) – that the gentry reacted to the events of the 1640s.

Unfortunately, much of the evidence on which historians have relied in writing the social history of the 1640s is intentionally misleading, either the deliberate polemic of both Royalists and Parliamentarians, who sought to raise the spectre of social revolution for their own ends, or the aspirations, but not achievements, of the radicals. It is therefore important to capture the balance between those changes which did seem to presage a social revolution and those limitations which help to explain the failure of a revolution within the revolution. We will look at the threat to the social order posed by a concatenation of disorder and a simultaneous questioning of the structures and ideas by which social order had been maintained. In a final section, we will examine why the 1640s did not in fact see the world turned upside down.

I

English gentlemen felt emboldened to challenge the King by the absence of popular rebellion in recent decades. The situation soon changed. The early 1640s was characterized by a level of crowd action which, in terms of the range of targets and geographical spread, had not been seen since the popular rebellions of 1549. The collapse of the personal rule of Charles I and the political vacuum created by the failure of Parliament and Crown to reach a settlement, gave scope for the people to settle their own grievances with unpopular landlords. The attack on the Crown and its supporters, labelled malignants and papists, offered legitimation for popular violence against the property and persons of those so labelled. The attack on the Laudian Church and the dismantling of its coercive apparatus gave similar scope for popular destruction in churches and attacks on Arminiam clergy. The raising of troops by King and Parliament collected the people together into armed bodies and enlarged the scope for popular action. Moreover, from the appeals to the country in the elections to Parliament to the continuing need for Parliament to counter the royal threat with public demonstrations of support, there was licence for crowds to assemble and protest.

*The pamphlets of the 1640s were full of visual as well as written
images of popular disturbances.*

The collapse of Charles's regime was the signal for widespread agrarian disorder. Riots, in which crowds of men, women and children assembled and tore down enclosures in defence of rights of common, took place in a number of counties. These were not a new form of action – indeed many of them represented the continuance of conflicts predating the 1640s – but what was new was the justification the rioters offered for their actions.

Star Chamber had been the court most involved in the prosecution of enclosure riots; its abolition left a vacuum which rioters exploited and which the House of Lords tried to fill. But orders from the House of Lords to cease rioting, when read out to crowds, were met with scorn and derision. Rioters in 1641 in the Lincolnshire fens said of such an order: 'They had believed too many orders of the higher house already . . . But if they had an Order from the House of Commons they would obey it.' Such declarations of support for the House of Commons may have been genuine, but they were paralleled by riots elsewhere in which crowds defied the attempts of magistrates to dismiss them on the pretext that since they were against the King, their authority had lapsed. 'Loyal' rioters in the Cambridgeshire fens told the magistrate attempting to disperse them, 'that he was no Justice, for he was against the King and was all for the Parliament'. Reports such as these suggested that rioters were deliberately and opportunistically exploiting the fracturing of political authority in their own interest to settle scores with enclosers. Thus, one rioter refused to obey an order of the Lords 'because his Majesty had declared that no ordinance of Parliament was to be obeyed without his Majesty's assent'.

Enclosure riots were not an indiscriminate attack on the landed classes. The overwhelming bulk of the riots were directed against those who were directly associated with the discredited *ancien régime* of Charles I: courtiers and city financiers who had sought to exploit links with the court to promote enclosure, enclosing bishops and, above all, Charles himself, whose direct involvement in the large-scale enclosure of royal forest and fen challenged the image of the King as protector of his people. But, synchronized by the collapse of authority at the centre and amplified by the attention given them in newsbooks, they seemed the first sign of the inundation of the vulgar the landed classes had always feared. Levelling of enclosures would, they feared, lead to levelling of society. When one MP in 1641 told his fellow MPs in a speech subsequently printed, 'we must take care that the Common people may not carve themselves out Justice, by their Multitudes. Of this we have too frequent experience by their breaking down Inclosures, and by raising other tumults, to as ill purposes . . . If they be not suddenly suppressed, to how desperate an Issue this may grow, I'll leave to your better judgements', he spoke to their common anxieties.

At the same time that they were carrying reports of agrarian disorders, the proliferating newsbooks also reported riots in churches against the changes Archbishop Laud had introduced. If anything, the pulling down of altar rails and images was more common that the pulling down of hedges. The rites of this popular iconoclasm reflected suspicion of Laud's seemingly 'popish' reforms and puritan hostility to his elevation of sacrament over sermon. Iconoclasts drew on Puritan preaching and a series of Parliamentary ordinances authorizing the dismantling of Laud's 'beauty of holiness' to sanction their actions. Moreover, iconoclasm was often carried out with the leadership or licence of local élites.

Iconoclasm, then, was not mindless violence. The rites of destruction reflected deeply-held beliefs and a sense of the legitimacy of their actions. For example, in the iconoclastic riots in Essex, images were taken to the traditional place of punishment and whipped. These distinctions were however lost on some contemporaries. Churches were the public meeting places of local society. As such, their seating plans often reflected local social hierarchies; the rich seated, the poor standing at the back of the church, men sitting separately from women and young people from their elders, all beneath the royal coat of arms. Churches were also temples to the gentry, many of whom held the right to appoint the minister. Their munificence was reflected in the heraldic displays on tomb and window. Iconoclasts were reported to destroy also the images of gentry thereby betraying, it was claimed, their hostility to their social superiors. In an ordinance of August 1643 calling for further alterations in churches, Parliament had to specify that the monuments of kings and nobles should not be destroyed. Ministers, as well as monuments, were attacked, their surplices (to Puritans, those 'rags of Rome') torn from their backs and the Common Prayer Book kicked from their hands. Royalist propagandists were quick to seize on and to exaggerate such incidents. Once again, popular disorder was linked with a threat to the social order. To many, even to committed Puritans, popular iconoclasm appeared to be 'abolishing superstition with sedition'.

That the people were becoming more politicized seemed to be confirmed by their role in the petitions and demonstrations that took place around Parliament's meeting in the early 1640s. On the one hand, the riots and demonstrations reflected popular hostility to many of the policies of the 1630s and fears of a popish conspiracy: the attack in 1640 on Laud's palace and the detested High Court, on Catholic embassies and chapels and the demonstrations against bishops, peers and the royal family. Again, many of these demonstrations were characterized by what one contemporary called a 'discipline in disorder'. The crowds often included wealthy citizens and acted on cues from Pym and his allies among London's preachers and politicians. The demonstrations were bloodless and contrasted sharply with the violence and lynchings that took place in similar movements on the Continent.

On the other hand, the large crowds that assembled around Parliament in 1640–2 reflected the poverty and unemployment that the political crisis had created, a situation that ran back from the capital and into the clothing regions, where many thousands depended upon London merchants for their market. Petitions and petitioners stressed their poverty. As the petition from the mayor and corporation of London told the Lords, depression would 'in a very short time cast innumerable Multitudes of those poor Men into such a Depth of Poverty and Extremity as will enforce them upon some dangerous and desperate Attempts not fit to be expressed, much less to be justified'. No wonder one gentleman on the occasion of the presentation of these petitions made notes in his private parliamentary journal about 'the great insurrection of the villeins and meaner people' in 1381. The 1640s witnessed coercive petitioning that showed scant respect or deference for social superiors, accompanied as it was by the manhandling of Lords and MPs. Even those who believed the people to be the ultimate basis of Parliament's authority, envisaged a passive rather than an active role in the polity for the people.

'Necessity hath no Law', 'hunger will break through stone walls', petitioners told Parliament. Riots in the provinces, as well as in London, seemed to offer dangerous confirmation of this observation. In 1642 it was reported from Suffolk that the unemployed clothworkers, 'begin to argue the case, whether in this great necessity it be not lawful, for to take something from those that have been the cause to deprive them of all manner of livelihood as to perish for hunger'. On the very eve of Civil War, large crowds in Essex and Suffolk, with underemployed clothworkers to the fore, had attacked and plundered the houses of local recusants and proto-Royalists amongst the nobility and gentry. Evidence suggests that these riots have a more complex history than the simple

Mercurius Rusticus

That Kings are the burdens and Plagues of those People or Nations over whom they govern. That the Relation of Masters and Servants hath no ground or warrant in the new Testament: but rather the contrary, for there we read, In Christ Jesus there is neither bond nor free, and we are all one in Christ. That the Honours and Titles of Dukes, Marquises, Earls, Viscounts, Lords, Knights and Gentlemen are but Ethnical and Heathenish distinctions, not to be retained amongst Christians. That one man should have a Thousand pounds a year, and another not one pound, perhaps not so much, but must live by the sweat of his brows, and must labour before he eat, hath no ground, neither in Nature or in Scripture. That the common People heretofore kept under blindness and Ignorance, have a long time yielded themselves Servants, nay slaves to the Nobility and the Gentry: but God hath now opened their eyes and discovered unto them their Christian liberty: and that therefore it is now fit that the Nobility and Gentry should serve their Servants, or at least work for their own maintenance; and if they will not work they ought not to eat.

*This report of the content of sermons preached in Chelmsford in the early 1640s comes from a hostile source, the royalist newsbook, Mercurius Rusticus, or the Countries Complaint of the Murthers, Robberies, Plundrings, and other Outrages, Committed by the Rebells on His Majesties faithfull Subjects. As its title clearly suggests this was a piece of deliberate propaganda designed to prove a causal link between Parliament's attack on the King and the broader threat to social hierarchies in the 1640s. Many, if not most, contemporaries would not have read it as propaganda. For the most part, gentlemen may have continued to live on reasonable terms with their own tenants and 'people', but it was dependence on sources like this for news of developments elsewhere that contributed to the 'moral panic' that gripped them.

Historians attempting to recover evidence about the beliefs of the people in the past (for a variety of reasons, one of the most difficult tasks facing them) have also found such sources seductive. But we need to keep in mind that, without other evidence, we cannot know whether such sermons were ever preached, or were exaggerated or even invented by Mercurius.

expression of class hostility that historians as well as contemporaries have taken them for. Such actions represented a popular response to the widely held fear of an internal rising of Catholics. The crowds produced what they took to be written Parliamentary authority for the disarming of proto-Royalists and Catholics. Elements of the middling sort joined the crowds, and members of the local Puritan and Parliamentary élite were (at least initially) not unhappy with crowd action that neutralized the incipient Royalist movement within the region.

Royalist propagandists, like the author of *Mercurius Rusticus*, were, however, quick to seize on the example of the East Anglian riots. The attention historians have devoted to them is a direct reflection of the notoriety they achieved with contemporaries. It was with these in mind that the Royalist Clarendon wrote of, 'the fury and license of the common people, who were in all places grown to that barbarity and rage against the nobility and gentry (under the style of *Cavaliers*) that it was not safe for any to live at their houses who were taken notice of as no votaries to the Parliament'. Elsewhere, for example in the West country, it was Parliamentarian gentry and Puritan ministers who found themselves menaced and mobbed. Once more, political divisions between Crown and Parliament legitimized attacks by inferiors on their superiors. Here indeed was a world turned upside down.

All the forms of disorder so far discussed tended to be concentrated in the period preceding the outbreak of Civil War. Thereafter they became less frequent, but they did not disappear entirely. Civil War created new sources of disorder. If anti-seigneurial riots had died down, the arrival of troops in a region might be the signal for local crowds to attack the property of unpopular landlords. The troops raised to fight the invading Scots had been active in pulling down hedges and altar rails. Some had attacked and killed several of their officers whom they had suspected of being Catholics; others had rioted over pay and attacked local Catholics. This was a thread of disorder that was to run through the 1640s as Parliament's soldiers desecrated cathedrals and pillaged Royalists and recusants. Royalist troops took similar action against the King's opponents. The foraging and quartering of poorly-paid troops probably provided a greater source of disorder in many regions. Discontent over feeding and paying troops was the background to the Clubmen risings in the mid-1640s, discontent over pay being one of the factors contributing to widespread mutinies and the emergence of the agitators in the New Model Army in 1647. The heavy cost of fighting the War forced the introduction of new and far heavier sources of tax. These too became sources of disorder. In particular, attempts to collect the excise, a tax which fell on essential foodstuffs, produced further riots. Harvest failures between 1647–9 brought a sharp intensification of poverty, a scattering of food riots and widespread discontent from which radicals like the Levellers and Diggers sought to recruit.

II

It was not just the multiplication of sources of collective disorder that threatened the social order. It was also the simultaneous changes in the structures of authority in Church and state *and* the challenge to the body of ideas by which the social order had been maintained.

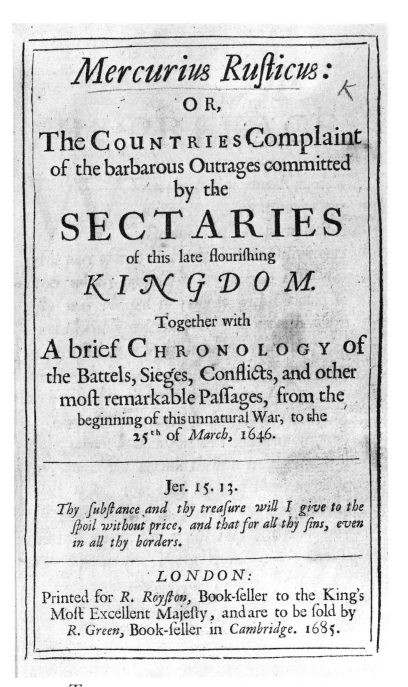

Mercurius Rusticus:

OR,

The COUNTRIES Complaint

of the barbarous Outrages committed

by the

SECTARIES

of this late flourishing

KINGDOM.

Together with

A brief CHRONOLOGY of
the Battels, Sieges, Conflicts, and other
moft remarkable Paffages, from the
beginning of this unnatural War, to the
25th of *March*, 1646.

Jer. 15. 13.

*Thy fubftance and thy treafure will I give to the
fpoil without price, and that for all thy fins, even
in all thy borders.*

LONDON:

Printed for *R. Royfton*, Book-feller to the King's
Moft Excellent Majefty, and are to be fold by
R. Green, Book-feller in *Cambridge.* 1685.

The title page of Mercurius Rusticus, *the most scurrilous and
effective of Royalist propaganda works, edited by Bruno Ryves.*

111

First, changes in the structures of authority. We have seen already how the collapse of conciliar government and the prerogative courts had made riots more difficult to prevent or punish. The House of Lords attempted to assume responsibility, but it (and the Commons even more so) tended to leave the resolution of disputes to 'the ordinary course of law'. But the circumstances of the 1640s meant that the course of law was more often extraordinary. The courts of assize and quarter sessions, courts of central importance in the maintenance of local order, ceased to meet (a gap of several years in some counties), while as we have seen, individual justices had their authority challenged. Worries over the source of their authority and difficulties of attendance in conditions of Civil War put obstacles in the way of using the remaining central courts.

Radicals challenged the entire basis of the legal system, individuals flouted its authority. The reported reply of a Wiltshire blacksmith to a woman seeking the return of her frying pan – 'she shall come by her pan as she can, for (saith he) there is no law' – would be amusing if it did not seem to reflect a wider belief. London watermen in 1641 had scorned the Lord Mayor's authority, 'boasting that they may do what they like (because now it is Parliament time)', while in 1649, a Somerset food rioter served with a justice's warrant, retorted 'that there was no law going nor no justice'. Manorial courts, by which the landed classes governed their estates were also disrupted by the absence of the lord or the seizure of the estates for political delinquency. This shifted power in favour of the tenants; one result was widespread rent strikes. It was such threats that encouraged a committed Parliamentarian like Sir Robert Harley to put properties before political interests and instruct his tenants to pay rents to the Royalists in possession of his estates.

New structures of state authority were created by the Civil War, but these with their heavy demands were seen as further sources of disorder. Moreover, in their recruitment of personnel from outside the ranks of the traditional ruling élite, county committees were themselves seen as socially subversive. Again, the reality is more complex. There were counties, for example Norfolk, Suffolk, Lancashire, where the old county élite remained in control of the county committee, but there were more counties – for example, Kent, Somerset, Warwickshire – where new and lesser gentlemen and townsmen came to govern the county. In general, the more strongly Royalist the county was and the later it fell to Parliament, the more sweeping were the changes in the social basis of power. By the end of the war the change in the social composition of both county committees and magistracy was more marked in most counties, even more so after the King's execution. This was hardly a social revolution. In most counties, as indeed in most corporations, the change was mainly *within* a class, from county to parochial gentry or wealthy merchant to merchant. Much of this change was what today we would call sponsored social mobility; elements of the old élite remained well represented among the new rulers of counties and cities. But, as the quotation from Sir John Oglander illustrating this chapter shows, such distinctions were lost on those contemporaries who yoked together the lower social status of the new rulers with their greater dependence on central powers to bolster their authority. Clarendon again captures the contemporary perception of an acutely status-conscious society in which power was expected to be as much a function of social status as office: 'a more inferior sort of the common people . . . who were not above the condition of ordinary inferior constables six to seven years before, were now the justices of the peace, sequestrators, and commissioners; who executed the commands of the Parliament in all the counties of the kingdom with such rigour and tyranny as was natural for such persons to use over and towards those upon whom they had formerly looked at such a distance'. Civil War armies, Parliamentarian and Royalist, saw non-gentry assuming command. This gave special affront in a society where the armed gentleman on horseback was a model for relationships of superiors with their biped inferiors. As in other periods war was a forcing house for social change. We should not allow comparisons with modern revolutions to blind us to the very real shock that the changes in the social relations of power delivered to such a hierarchical society. The Colonel Pride who purged a Parliament of landowners was a former drayman.

New policies as well as new rulers disturbed traditional patterns of authority. Parliament enlisted the co-operation of the people in the implementation of its policies. It was from the well-affected amongst the 'middling sort' – yeomen farmers, merchants and master craftsmen – that Parliament recruited local office-holders. (Evidence suggests a similar process in areas under Royalist administration.) This was a trend that long pre-dated the 1640s, but then the 'middling sort' had implemented the directives of gentlemen magistrates, attempting at the same time to act as brokers for the interests of their local communities in mitigating the impact of those directives. Now they were being asked to enforce central policies against local gentlemen and communities. At the same time these policies gave official licence to subordinates to testify against their social superiors. The process of sequestration gave tenants the opportunity to depose against landlords; the committees for scandalous ministers required parishioners to inform against their minister.

Not only élites were affected. Those who had seen the struggle as one for godly reformation were now able to pass ordinances with the aim of reforming a popular culture they regarded as superstitious and sinful. Godly magistrates and their allies among the middling sort sought to curb the alehouse and the role of drinking in popular sociability, to restrict the number of holidays and festivities and to reform customary forms of sexual behaviour and marriage formation. Social values as well as relationships were challenged in the 1640s. The hostility this attempted cultural revolution provoked was reflected in the extent to which the calendar and customs of popular culture became occasions for protest against the Parliamentary regime and its officials.

The toppling of the traditional structures of authority within the Church also had consequences for society. The demise of bishops and the Church courts seemed to coincide with the rise of separatist religious groups, whose doctrines carried radical social as well as religious implications. Separatist congregations emerged which stressed a spiritual equality that justified preaching and prophesying by the laity. In rejecting the distinction between laity and clergy, and in denying the need for an Established Church, they were threatening both the gentry's and middling sort's control of the parish.

Gender as well as social hierarchies were challenged by the emergence of the sects. Sects, in which women often outnumbered men, gave women a far more active public role. Within the sects they were allowed to debate and vote. Some

THE
Parliament of VVomen.

220

With the merrie Lawes by them newly
Enacted. To live in more Eafe, Pompe, Pride,
and wantonneffe : but efpecially that they might have fu-
periority and domineere over their husbands ; with a new way
found out by them to cure any old or new Cuckolds, and
how both parties may recover their credit
and honefty againe

Londen, Printed for *W.Wilfon* and are to be fold by him in
Will-yard in Little Saint *Bartholomewes.* 1646.

Aug: 14 : London 1646.

*T*he sense of inverted values extended to fears of
inverted gender roles.

sects, it was alleged, gave women the right to preach; by exploiting contemporary notions of the nature of female spiritual power to prophesy, women claimed this right for themselves. At the same time, the collapse of censorship allowed women to write and publish tracts in unprecedented numbers. Some women played a more active public political role, organizing petitions and mobilizing support for the Levellers. By 1649, *The Humble Petition of Divers Well-Affected Women* could justify women's new role in the following language: 'we are assured of our creation in the image of God, and of an interest in Christ, equal unto men, as also of a proportionable share in the Freedoms of this Commonwealth'.

The correspondence between authority in the state and the authoritarian patriarchal relationship between husband and wife in the 'little commonwealth' of the family was central to early modern political culture. It suggested that the political authority of the King and the domestic authority of the husband were validated both by God and nature. The fifth commandment – honour thy father and mother – was a key text in the prescription of obedience and deference in political, social and domestic relationships. As a Presbyterian critic of the sects warned, fathers 'should never have peace in their families more, or ever after have command of wives, children or servants'. Lurid tales of sexual delinquency among the sects suggested that spiritual liberty threatened carnal licence. With an active debate on marriage and calls for divorce, the family itself seemed threatened. The sexual as well as the social order was under threat in the 1640s.

Religious and political controversy threatened all those whose authority was grounded in respect for their social status. Perhaps the most worrying way this was brought home to contemporaries is to historians the most elusive: changes in language and social grammar, those central markers of any social order. The deference of social subordinates to their superiors in early modern society was marked by a series of everyday social rituals in speech and body language. For example, subordinates bared their head and stood in the presence of their superiors; in addressing them they used terms of respect. These were important as unconscious but powerful acknowledgements of the 'natural' superiority of their 'betters' within the social order. Civil War (which itself institutionalized plebeian attacks on their betters, something hitherto denied by the code of the duel) saw this etiquette breached and disregarded and, worse still, parodied in rites of subversive humour by sects and soldiers among others. The landed classes found both their social space and social distance invaded. We do not yet know how common this was – the history of the challenge to social convention has yet to be written – but the threat this was thought to pose can be gauged by the severity of the later reaction to the Quakers, who refused to use the respectful second person plural of 'you' to superiors (using the familiar 'thou' instead) or to 'cap' them.

More worryingly still, the spiritual equality of the priesthood of believers might turn into the brotherhood of Man. Levellers like John Lilburne had been schooled in the separatist groups of London; the Leveller movement crystallized out of the struggle for religious toleration. The Cheshire gentleman, Sir Thomas Aston, feared, 'the old seditious argument, that we are the sons of Adam, born free, some of them say, the Gospel hath made them free . . . They will plead Scripture for it, that we should all live by the sweat of our brows'.

Troubled conservatives saw the collapse of morality as well as of political structures.

'People are governed more by the pulpit than the sword in times of peace,' Charles I had declared. This was a statement that could be applied to many early modern states, but it applied with particular force to England where the absence of army and police had meant that the authority of both the King and the landed classes rested on consent rather than coercion. It was the public challenge to the ideological hegemony by which English society had been ordered that made the multiple forms of disorder in the 1640s threatening. New and radical intentions might lie behind the traditional form of the enclosure or food riot.

A Royalist Lament

I believe such times were never before seen in England, when the gentry were made slaves to the commonalty and in their power, not only to abuse but plunder any gentleman. No law and government, no assizes, no sessions, no justices that would be obeyed, no spiritual courts . . . [Gentlemen] could call nothing their own and lived in slavery and submission to the unruly, base multitude . . . We had a thing here called a Committee, which over-ruled Deputy Lieutenants and also Justices of the Peace, and of this we had brave men: Ringwood of Newport, the pedlar; Maynard, the apothecary; Matthews the baker; Wavell and Legge, farmers, and poor Baxter of Hurst Castle. These ruled the whole Island and did whatsoever they thought good in their own eyes.

This lament from the commonplace notebook of Sir John Oglander, a Royalist, captures the reaction of England's traditional rulers, the landed gentry, to the changes in the social bases of power that the 1640s brought. The social changes were often not as great as Sir John's comments would suggest, but his mixture of outrage and contempt reflects the dominant assumption that it was the gentry's right to rule since land commanded greater respect than trade or commerce. Perhaps only gentlemen with a fierce commitment to Puritanism were able to ignore these traditional assumptions.

The centrality of enclosure as a metaphor for social and political order in the discourse of the 1640s made the throwing down of hedges a social and political threat; it was this that made Charles I's labelling of the Levellers by the name of earlier agrarian rebels such an effective smear. In the dearth of 1649, the Wiltshire justices were the recipients of a petition which blamed their own greed for the high food prices. Earlier in the decade, one Parliamentarian (with estates at the heart of the East Anglian riots) had confided to his journal, 'there is no doubt but that all right and property all *meum* and *tuum* [mine and thine] must cease in civil wars: & we know not what advantage the meaner sort also may take to divide the spoils of the rich and noble amongst them, who begin already to allege, that all being of one mould there is no reason that some should have so much and others so little'. When Adam delved and Eve span, who was then the gentleman?

III
With all sources of authority challenged in a society with long-term stresses exacerbated by the pressures of Civil War and the challenge of radical ideas, it did indeed seem that the world might be turned upside down. In 1649, the King was executed and monarchy, along with the House of Lords and episcopacy, was abolished. Ideas in circulation, and the radical groups that sought to implement them, offered a challenge to all traditional sources of authority. But the world was not turned upside down; the radicals were defeated and many of their ideas

117

*An allegory of regicide: the King is being thrown overboard;
lightning strikes St Stephen's Chapel (the House of Commons); and
anarchy breaks out amongst the people as the army stands by.*

failed to gain general acceptance. Previously, the death of the monarch had been the signal for an upsurge in disorder reflecting the popular belief that until a new King was proclaimed, or crowned, there was no law. But in 1649 the death of monarchy did not see any such increase in disorder. Why was this?

For a start, we need to repeat that much of the evidence that the historian is forced to rely on exaggerates the threat of social upheaval. With the certainties of their world collapsing around them, propertied contemporaries were in the grip of a moral panic. Their fears were fed by the unprecedented spate of cheap pamphlets and newsletters and the propaganda of both Royalists and Parliamentarians.

Second, viewed through the distorting prism of political polemic and their own fears, the threat radical groups and the sects posed was exaggerated. Most sects sought an equality of *souls*, not society. In 1647 the London Independents issued a declaration which sought to disassociate themselves from the Leveller programme: 'it cannot but be very prejudicial to human society, and the promotion of the good of the Commonwealth, Cities, Armies, or families, to admit of a parity, or all to be equal in power', they declared. 'The ranging of men into several and subordinate ranks and degrees is a thing necessary for the good of them'. Many Independent congregations were disciplinarian, rather than libertarian, retaining a desire for a looser form of national Church able to reform the profane multitude. They sought godly reformation, not social revolution.

The World Turned Upside Down

To these doctrines you may join their practice. The seditious Pamphlets, the tumultuous rising of rude multitudes threatening blood and destruction, the preaching of cobblers, feltmakers, tailors, grooms, and women, the choosing of any place for God's service but the Church; the night meetings of naked men and women; the licentiousness of spiritual marriages without any legal form. These things, if they be not looked unto, will bring us in time to community of wives, community of goods, and destruction of all.

★*A Short History of the Anabaptists of High and Low Germany* pamphlet published in London, May 1642. This pamphlet which purports to tell the history of the radical movements within the German Revolt of 1525, is in reality an attempt to equate developments in England (to which this extract refers) with the bloody and lurid history of the later stages of that earlier movement of social protest. Anabaptists, their doctrines mangled and misrepresented, had become the bogeymen of the propertied classes in early modern Europe. Anabaptism, as the frequency with which it was referred to in the 1640s shows, was a convenient label to pin on those who sought reform, however limited. Such labelling suggested that reform would become revolution, in the sexual as well as the social order. As such it threatened all holders of traditional authority, all the way down to husbands.

Nor was the threat to gender hierarchies as great as supposed. While some sects agreed that the duty of women to obey their conscience justified disobeying fathers and husbands, they restricted this to spiritual matters, acknowledging that 'in bodily and civil respects' the husband still had authority. (Of course, in practice, the distinction may have been harder to make.) Even within the sects ambiguities remained over the legitimacy of women's speaking, and it became clear that *within* the group, patriarchal authority was to be observed. That the Levellers in the Putney debates claimed the vote for the 'poorest *he*' reflects the strength of patriarchal assumptions even amongst the radicals, accepted also (at least in public) by their female supporters.

Third, the exceptional conditions of the 1640s allowed ideas to circulate freely, but their acceptance was more difficult, collective action upon them even more so. The radicals of the mid-seventeenth century did not form revolutionary vanguard parties. Impressive though their organization was by seventeenth-century standards, it was restricted to certain areas and their programmes, betraying their religious origins and belief in the power of God-given reason, and relied more on moral than physical force. As we have seen, the ideas of the sects were as likely to attract popular (as well as élite) enmity as much as enthusiasm. We should be careful not to conflate the radical with the popular. They were a minority, an important one, but a minority still. It was only in certain types of physical and social space within the revolution that people were able to organize and act on radical ideas: the New Model army, areas of forest and pasture with the absence of a resident gentry, the presence of the cloth industry and an earlier tradition of radicalism and, above all London (though even here work in progress suggests that the structures of local government presented an obstacle to the more radical types of reform).

This is the fourth, and perhaps most important point. If we view events from the centre then the emphasis is on conflict. But seen from the counties there is increasing evidence of continuity. Long-term changes created instability, but they also helped create the structures with which to contain instability. At the level of the village, where most of the population lived, economic change had promoted a process of social differentiation. Increasingly, this had aligned the wealthier yeomen farmers – the 'middling sort' – with the gentry. It had distanced them from their poorer neighbours and encouraged them, through holding local office, to co-operate in the extension of the power of the state at the local level, a process best reflected in their increasing use of the criminal courts and implementation of an effective poor law to curb the threat of the poor.

The re-alignment of social forces (which had its parallels in urban society) meant that these powerful local élites were unlikely to welcome schemes that challenged the economic order from which they drew their wealth. They approached the revolution Janus-faced. They were concerned to defend their property and faith against royal absolutism and episcopal Arminianism and, for some, to assert their social status against the old élite. But they were also anxious not to see these threatened from below, hence for some, the added appeal of a disciplinary Calvinism. At the same time, the loss of land by the poorer sort, where it occurred, was making them dependent on these local village élites for employment and relief. Here at the most local level was a social structure that was able to cope with the crises of the later 1640s and prevent the widespread suffering that might have mobilized the 'many-headed monster' by continuity in the implementation of an effective system of poor relief. Significantly, in the difficult 1640s grain riots were less frequent. But this was also a system which could penalize too open an expression of support for radical ideas. The radical Roger Crabbe showed an appreciation of these realities when he wrote of 'labouring poor Men, which in Times of scarcity pine and murmur for want of Bread, cursing the Rich behind his Back, and before his Face, Cap, and Knee'. It was no coincidence that radical ideas and groups were most likely to be found in areas where the powers of landlord, minister, magistrate and middling sort might be weaker: fen and forest, rural industrial areas and the larger cities.

The consequences of this re-alignment of social forces in the countryside can be illustrated by returning to the example of enclosure riots. Historians, like contemporaries, have been impressed by the extent of enclosure riots in the 1640s. But there is evidence to suggest that they were less threatening than has been supposed. The 1640s did not see a general rising of the countryside. What is striking about agrarian disorder in the 1640s is its absence from many areas. For example, enclosure riots had been earlier most frequent in the Midlands and the region had in 1607 experienced the largest agrarian rising by groups styling themselves Levellers and Diggers. But there were very few riots here in the 1640s. The absence of enclosure riots from many areas is testimony to the growing alliance between landlords and tenants in the development of agrarian capitalism. This replaced social solidarity between yeomen and the poorer sort with social distance and denied discontented smallholders and cottagers the leadership they required to translate rural discontent into collective action. It was in the forests of the South-West and the fens of Eastern England that enclosure riots were concentrated, areas where social differentiation was less pronounced and where middling and poorer sort shared a common hostility to sweeping enclosure imposed from outside.

Despite some examples, well publicized by Royalist propaganda, of crowds destroying manorial records, most riots represented the continuation of an earlier tradition of agrarian protest. In the main, enclosure riots did not reflect the demand for access to land based on natural rights, but a more restricted claim to common rights within the manorial system on which landlord power was based. As the hostility to the King in areas with direct experience of royal enclosure showed, there was potential for formal politicization, but this failed to materialize. Parliament's decision to assume responsibility for protecting the property of enclosers and its failure to enfranchise copyholders ensured that land and liberty would not become the official slogans of this revolution. The radical groups later in the 1640s failed to provide either an effective programme or leadership for rural discontent. The Levellers, reflecting their urban origins, never gave sufficient attention to enclosure, and they remained primarily an urban-based movement. The Diggers gave greater attention to the land question, but their scheme for collective cultivation of the waste ran counter to the existing tradition of the protection of common rights to uphold shrinking individual holdings. Local communities had not fought lords of the manor to protect their rights only to surrender them to the Diggers. Enclosure rioters attacked landlords, not landlordism. They sought rights of common, not rights for the Commons of England.

The failure of the singlest largest social group in seventeenth-century England, the rural poor, to rise reflects the importance of the underlying social transformation which made the 'middling sort' bulwarks of local order in the midst of political crisis. In fact the period of the 1640s and 1650s marks an important transition in the way order was maintained at a local level. Before 1640 there had been an unprecedented use of the courts to prosecute the poor; later in the seventeenth century the courts became less important as the local economic and social power allowed the middling sort to discipline the poor without formal use of the courts. Men may have been worried in the 1640s by the (temporary) absence of courts, but there is evidence to suggest that the new social relationships of power within most communities were capable of containing the threat.

IV

The emphasis here on the threat the 1640s brought to the social order should not be allowed to exclude the other social face of the 1640s. Not everybody regarded the 1640s as signalling an impending confusion. For many these were days of liberty and liberation. For committed Parliamentarians and godly Puritans this was a decade of reform. While one gentleman scribbled notes in his Parliamentary diary about 1381, another wrote 'no time nor history can show that such great numbers of oppressed Subjects of all sorts ever petitioned with that humility and dissolved so quietly'. The extant notebooks of the London woodturner Nehemiah Wallington provide ample testimony of the hopes of humbler Puritans. For him, the acts of iconoclasm he so carefully chronicled were not evidence of the 'reforming rabble' but of godly reformation. In the provinces, committed Puritans like Richard Baxter welcomed the chance to build a holy commonwealth. For the radicals and their supporters, the progress of the decade brought the possibility of a revolution in Man's relationship both with God and with fellow men and women. It is impossible to do justice to the ferment of ideas this unleashed or the sense of freedom this brought to many men *and* women.

The emphasis here has been on the threat developments in the 1640s were thought to pose to the social order because ultimately this had the greater significance for the history of the period. Historical analysis might be able to demonstrate (not without a generous dose of hindsight on the part of the historian) that the chances of a radical threat to the social order in the 1640s were more limited than contemporaries supposed, but it was contemporaries' perceptions of the reality of that threat upon which they acted. In 1649, 'the year of intended parity' according to one pamphleteer, few could have been confident that the social order would not be subverted. It was this fear of social upheaval that created the 'party of order' which allowed Charles to fight a Civil War and encouraged men of property in increasing numbers to urge a negotiated settlement. It was the same fear that encouraged a *de facto* acceptance of the Cromwellian regime and that regime's failure to guarantee order that led to the Restoration and the righting of a world turned upside down.

CHAPTER VII

The Impact on Literature

PETER THOMAS

I

'**A**rms and the Man I Sing' – so Virgil proclaimed, from the heart of Rome's Augustan peace, poetry's epic bond with war. Down the ages that bond has endured. Even the apocalyptic horrors of the Somme in 1916, when the noise of history's greatest and most terrible pitched battle could be heard in England and a million men were killed, could not cancel it. For men march away to war armed not just with swords or guns, but myths and potent images as well. So world-conquering Alexander took 'dead Homer with him to the battlefield'; and Sir Philip Sidney pondered the paradox that poetry (one of the arts of peace) 'in England flourished even at the time when the trumpet of Mars did sound loudest'. In 1914–18 when Mars had his field day, so did the pen.

So it was with Britain's Civil War. A far cry, of course, from the carnage of armies bogged down across Europe. Barbed wire, poison gas, machine guns and howitzers hour after hour showering high explosives were a long way off. Nor was there, save in Ireland, anything that came near the savagery of the Thirty Years War. But musket and cannon, sword, pike and pistol did their work; and many tens of thousands were slain or maimed. After Marston Moor bodies were strewn for miles along the way to York. Marching armies, pitched battles, innumerable skirmishes, sieges and storms left their trail of damage across the land. And the sights and sounds of an unnatural war on native soil became embedded in the mental landscape. For though the Wars of the Roses had lived on in literature as a warning, Britain had long become, in Samuel Daniel's phrase, 'a wonder to other lands', its violent past essentially a prelude to the unique peace and plenty of Stuart rule. The noise of drum and trumpet faded. There was no standing army. The sea seemed sufficient defence. Albion by 1637 was, in George Daniel's words, a 'Great and Glorious Isle', green and blessed, a garden redeemed from history.

There were other voices, of course: no nation is ever altogether satisfied. Some complained that people were 'besotted' with peace; others called for battle in the name of solidarity with European Protestants. Antichrist was not beaten yet. Indeed, the zealous spied his hand in Caroline appeasement and creeping popery. And books like Joseph Mede's 1632 *Key to Revelation* (enough of Armageddon and prophetic history there for anyone) fanned the flames, if not of war then of millenarian politics.

Still, Laud and Strafford seemed to have things in hand; the government was solvent and solid, and at the centre Charles and Henrietta Maria presided over the Court of Love and Beauty. The muses, rejoiced Thomas Carew, were at home amidst these modest shades, the 'myrtle bowers' where Daphne sings not

Some Terms and Dates

APOCALYPTIC revelatory, like the grand and violent events prophesied in St John's *Book of Revelation*, a key text of the century, widely used as a literary and political model.

CAIN the first fratricide and murderer, condemned to live a fugitive and vagabond.

FAST SERMONS not swift, but delivered on days of humiliation and thanksgiving, and published by order of the Commons or Lords.

FIRST BISHOPS WAR in 1639 provoked by the attempt of Charles I to impose Anglicanism on Scotland. It ended inconclusively.

HERMETIC of alchemy or other occult sciences, after 'Hermes Tris-megistus', supposed founder of these sciences.

MILLENARIAN relating to the millenium, i.e. the 1,000 years of Christ's Kingdom on earth. The Civil War and Regicide were commonly inter-preted as heralding that final renovation.

PHAETON in Greek mythology, the driver of the sun-chariot who by rash, over-adventurous driving set the world on fire.

PINDARIC irregular verse, after the Greek poet Pindar, whose odes permitted a degree of metrical variety and freedom.

RAIL a small wading bird.

THEOCRATS advocates of government by God directly or through a priestly order.

TUCK a rapier.

Odysseus's 'dull dream' of adventure, but 'Sweet odes of love, such as deserve the bays'. Naturally there is always the 'obdurate' rabble in the wings; and the 'Genevan Drum' bellowing 'for freedom and revenge' makes noises off. But 'Halcyon Days' are here to stay. The King's Arcadia, this 'secure fix'd state', has no need of Gustavus Adophus's Protestant heroics. Carew, mocking the code that would have him fight and kill, was happy to settle for less than epic.

Not until the King marched on Scotland – and lost – did the idyll unravel. Retreating from the First Bishops War, Carew found Arcadia still intact in his friend's country estate. But the framing images of his poem *To G.N. from Wrest*, while insulating the place from without, convey discomfiture. The poet saw war closing in. Too soon, though he was dead by then, his worst fears for poetry were confirmed. The 1640s brought a rude awakening. The opposing armies of a divided nation 'deflowered the groves', driving the muses from their lyric shade. No avoiding now the larger, more public, political strains Carew jibbed at. Andrew Marvell's *Nymph complaining*,

> The wanton troopers riding by
> Have shot my fawn and it must die,

contrived to sustain something of the old note, but registered unflinchingly the betrayal, casual brutality and heartbreak. Violence had broken in, forcing us from a harmless halcyon past towards the wilderness. Not even nymphs can stand aside from history. The 'forward youth' of Marvell's *An Horatian Ode* (1650) has the same painful growing-up to do: he must

> . . . forsake his muses dear
> Nor in the shadows sing
> His numbers languishing

but sally forth armed into the unknown. So Marvell, accepting destiny, a decade on decisively reverses Carew's gestures.

II

Once Civil War broke out there was no escaping the facts. From 1640 the country was awash with news. Censorship had hitherto prevented the publication of all but foreign and harmless home-grown stories: henceforth pamphlets and periodicals poured from the presses. The list is endless: *A Bloudy Fight* here; *A Great Victory* there. Here *Good Newes*, *Joyfull Newes*, *Exceeding Joyfull Newes*; there *Bad Newes*, *Bloudy Newes*, *Horrible Newes*, *Strange Newes*. *Mercurius Aulicus* appears weekly for the Court; *Britanicus* for Parliament. And every week *Diurnalls*, *Occurrences*, *Passages*, *Accompts*, *Intelligencers*, *Messengers*, *Informers*, *Scouts*, *Posts*, *Proceedings* issued forth. Some were short-lived; some, like *The Kingdomes Weekly Intelligencer* (1642–9) kept going for years.

There were printed Sermons and Speeches aplenty, along with Votes, Acts and Ordinances, Proclamations, Motions, Resolutions, Remonstrances, and Relations; Petitions, Propositions, Prospectuses and Protestations; Animadversions, Answers, Arguments, Reasons, Relations and Replies; Observations, Examinations, Vindications, Queries and Questions, Confutations and Complaints, Catalogues and Collections; Advertisements, Almanacs, Charters, Discoveries, Elegies, Epistles, Intelligences, Libels, Panegyrics, Memorials, Narrations, Poems, Plays, Romances, Satires, Treatises of all shapes and sizes. The printed word went everywhere. Journalism and party propaganda came of age. Heroically, London publisher George Thomason collected everything he could, amounting, over 20 years, to some 20,000 items, – 'the most valuable set of documents', thundered Carlyle, 'connected with English history'. There had never been anything before to compare with this war of words. It was an information revolution.

As for the war of swords, the ramshackle armies needed licking into shape, and both sides issued laws and ordinances to that end. Impressive-looking lists of officers, and commanders' engraved portraits (often triumphantly equestrian) were printed. Drill manuals for pikemen and musketeers – there were even indecent parodies of such things – and treatises on artillery operations proliferated, many highly technical and illustrated. And around the battles, sieges and skirmishes, pamphlets and newsbook reports crowded and clustered, mapping the shifting scene of an embattled land. The fighting soon forced itself on almanacs: once habitually deferential to government, by 1644, commenting on and predicting events, they mirrored the entrenched antagonisms. Both sides invoked the stars: Parliament looked to John Booker and William Lilly; the Royalists to George Wharton – 'A huge rot'n rogue' to his anagrammatizing enemies! Almanacs, like the abundant popular ballads and broadsheets, insist-

Pag: 1007

MERCVRIVS AVLICVS,

Communicating the Intelligence and affaires of the Court, to the reft of the KINGDOME.

The 23 *VVeeke, ending* June 8. 1644.

SUNDAY. *June* 2.

His day began ill, but it ended well. For the firft newes of the morning was, that *Waller* had the day before attempted once againe to obteine the paffage at *Newbridge*, which was maintained againft him by 90 musketteirs as long as their powder and fhot lafted. But that begining to be fpent towards the evening, before the new fupply which was fent came to them, the *Rebells* had got over the water in Bôates at a little diftance from the Bridge, and falling fuddainly upon them killed and tooke prifoners 30 of them or thereabouts. But this ill newes was recompenfed with the good fucceffe which His Majefties forces had the laft night at *Gofworth* Bridge, where they killed an hundred of the *Rebels*, as before I told you: it being credibly reported that the *Rebells* had carried away 3 Cart loades of their dead men, befides thofe whom they left in the ditches, whom they had not the courage to fetch off. And to make up the number of thofe men which were loft and taken by Sir *William* yefterday, there came this day unto His Majefties Army, 40. Dutch Troopers more who had ferved the Enemy.

q q   But

*T*he cover of one of the dozens of newspapers (many ephemeral) that were spawned by the Civil War.

ently deepened political awareness and the apocalyptic atmosphere. A nation pored avidly over the entrails and omens.

Sometimes the very layout of broadsheets confronts readers with conflict and choice, as when *The Two Incomparable Generalissimos of the World* (Satan and Christ) are drawn up facing us in two vertical columns of verse. Binary oppositions may be perennial in nature and the psyche, but in the 1640s they sprang, as never before, fully armed from the page. Inevitably there were horror stories, as of the wounded Parliamentary soldier at Arundel Castle 'hewed . . . all to peeces'; and lucky escapes, like Michael Woodhead's who was 'shot upon his tin buttons, his doublet burst neare the heart, and the bruised bullet fell down into his breeches and no hurt'. Other survivors were less fortunate: Mr Tillen shot standing in his doorway, had his leg and thighbone broken. Another was run through the buttocks with a tuck. Mr Richard Cave lost both his eyes at Marston Moor. The list is endless and remarkably matter-of-fact. 'When Leggs and Armes did quarrell in the Air, shot off from maimed bodies' sounds like literary hyperbole; but it is underwritten by the laconic memoir of the London trooper who found it 'somewhat dreadful when men's bowels and braines flew in our faces'. Similarly, 'The parted Head hung downe on either Side' in Abraham Cowley's three-book unfinished epic *The Civil War* comes not from his Classical or Biblical sources, but straight from the Battle of Newbury.

The scene at 'popish' Basing Castle when it fell to Cromwell's psalm-singing army, was no less grim. To Hugh Peter, his chaplain, reporting to the Commons, the storming, putting to the sword, looting and burning, even the men entombed in the debris of a tower, were a necessary desolation on the march to final renovation. He made much of it, not least of the moment when Inigo Jones, presiding genius of Caroline masques, was carted out of the ruins naked, wrapped in a blanket. The spell of court ritual lay broken beneath the heel of *Revelation*.

To say two idioms collided sounds, amidst so much tangible destruction, absurdly academic. Both armies, after all, saw themselves as Christians fighting under God's providence. Prayers and worship of one sort or another were the rule in both camps, and both heard sermons before Marston Moor. But the modest serviceable note on the King's side is startlingly different from William Dell's prophetic millenarian harangue on the other. There is no mistaking the quarrel over meaning. The Kingdom of God was *not* the same on both sides of the fence. John Bastwick in *The Storming of the Anabaptists Garrisons* (1647) (the title sounds saleable) reproached sectarians for being overfond of military terminology. The Fast Sermons to Parliament (488 of them delivered between 1640 and 1653) are peppered with the word of war, with not a little dashing of brains and sheathing of righteous swords in the bowels of the enemy. The godly insist on the 'quarrell . . . betwixt Christ and Antichrist' as part of their distinctive identity. They wore it like a badge. So in and out of battle they forged an idiom to overpower the enemy. With pen and sword, abandoning the old ideal of national unanimity, they forced division and the visionary onto the agenda of politics and literature.

George Wither's *Campo Musae* (1643) says it all. Through 70 rambling pages of verse it weaves together vivid documentary, political and moral commentary, and prophetic rhapsodizing. We find ourselves in the field and inside the head

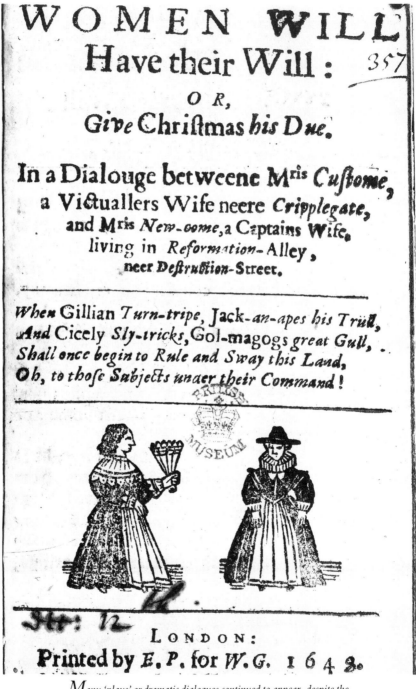

WOMEN WILL
Have their Will: 357
OR,
Give Christmas his Due.

In a Dialouge betweene Mris *Custome*,
a Victuallers Wife neere *Cripplegate*,
and Mris *New-oome*, a Captains Wife,
living in *Reformation*-Alley,
neer *Destruction*-Street.

When Gillian *Turn-tripe*, Jack-an-apes his *Trull*,
And Cicely *Sly-tricks*, Gol-magogs great *Gull*,
Shall once begin to Rule and Sway this Land,
Oh, to those Subjects under their Command!

Str: 12

LONDON:
Printed by *E. P.* for *W. G.* 1648.

*M*any 'plays' or dramatic dialogues continued to appear, despite the
closing of the theatres by the Puritans.

128

of a soldier who knew (to borrow Cromwell's formulation) what he fought for and loved what he knew. And there is, first impressions notwithstanding, method in his madness. Wither was an accomplished craftsman, and the mix and sudden *démarches* of his 'distractive musings' derived from the Puritan confessional mode and were shaped by the 'Interruptions and Confusions of War'. There is no place in 'Destructive Times' for poetic invocations (which true-blue Puritanism eschewed) or for well-rounded endings. The poem simply comes to a halt in haste to horse at morning trumpet call. The fighting dictates everything now, even the shape of poetry – as Abraham Cowley found on the other side when defeat stopped his triumphal epic in its tracks. No wonder he concluded that 'a warlike, various, and a tragical age is best to write of, but worst to write in'. There is no more authentic image of the Civil War felt on the pulse than Wither's *Campo Musae*, warts and all! Nor any more moving lament for the 'pleasant arbours, hackt and hewd'

> Through Walks and Fields, which I have visited
> With peacefull Mates, and free from fear of harmes;
> Yea, there, where oft Faire ladies I have led,
> I now lead on, a Troupe of men in Armes.
> In Meadowes, where our sports were wont to be
> (And where we playing wantonly have laine)
> Men sprawling in their blood, we now do see:
> Grim postures, of the dying, and the slaine.

No Hugh Peter-like rejoicing here, for all Wither's longing after building a new 'Jerusalem'; but something closer-kin to William Blake. Wither had cherished the pastoral mode in Jacobean days and lived, a small landowner, to have his estate plundered, and to fight back. Arcadia was not, after all, the sole property of Court, but part of the freeborn Englishman's landscape. The desecration now – and the damage done to fields, crops and houses was not negligible – is the *coup de grâce* to the old identity and wholeness. The ground, a real and imagined place which had defined men's sense of self, was blasted. Worst of all, it was a self-inflicted injury:

> Our selves, against our selves we strongly arme.

It is not just that Englishmen are slaughtering each other in a war that they cannot, by definition, win: Wither's words, knowingly or not, register a profounder self-division too, a deep inward collision and split that have occurred. John Quarles's 'My thoughts surprise my thoughts' and Marvell's image of the self-mown mower confirm the diagnosis.

The dislocations of *Campo Musae*, as Wither struggles to internalize the Civil War, and re-form and re-connect his inner and outer worlds, are telling. So, in its very different way, is *Aqua Musae* (1645), John Taylor's satiric riposte, sending up Wither's warlike inspirations and his military pretensions, with his jargon of 'Ambuscadoes' and 'Pallisadoes'. Wither is all 'Contradiction' and 'Nonsense'.

More sobering, however, is the sense of betrayal of one popular and prolific poet by another. Taylor had loved and respected 'Honest George Wither' for 35 years: now he must construe him 'Hypocrite'. Lacking Wither's insight, Taylor confirms the loss of shared meaning, the confusion of categories. Words can no longer be trusted: they mean different things depending where you stand. In Taylor's public falling-out with Wither the struggle to possess the language and the land (in which Thomas Hobbes's *Leviathan*, purging ambiguities, would later so massively intervene) is palpable. Division and doubleness drove deep into art and life. Looking back, Cowley's image of the parted skull becomes, though otherwise intended, the perfect emblem of the times.

III

Amidst all this, the poetic muse still flourished, or at least was still published in the 1640s. Carew, Waller, Suckling, Shirley, Hall, Cowley, Herrick, Lovelace, Crashaw, Vaughan, Milton make it look like lyrics' heyday. It is an illusion. Most of Carew's, Herrick's and Waller's verse was composed in the 1620s and 1630s. Milton's compositions, too, belong to the Caroline world, courtly and aristocratic. His prose polemics of the 1640s were played down in publisher Humphrey Moseley's talk of 'evergreen and not to be blasted laurels'. Moseley masterminded most of these volumes not for profit or memorial alone, but to sustain a sense of literary community despite the unsettlement of patronage and audience. In the nick of time, a body of primarily private, coterie verse was brought into the public arena. War brings some benefits!

The times, nonetheless, *were* out of tune. All seems well at first in Herrick's *Hesperides*; but discordant notes creep in among the lovely incantations, growing signs of fragmentation. 'Lost is Musicke now', and 'publick ruine bears down all'. Then the mood swings: the poet sings on 'unamaz'd', defiantly trusting to 'good verses'. Charles, under house-arrest at Hampton Court, is 'great Augustus' still. Richard Lovelace, who knew what it meant when 'there's nothing you can call your own', saw things differently. His King at Hampton Court (in the poem on Peter Lely's portrait of Charles with his second son James) is no Augustus. More like a martyr-in-waiting. Catching 'clouded majesty', 'happy misery', 'sad contempt', 'victorious sorrow', the painter draws Charles as a self-sufficient, loving Christian stoic. The era of kingly ikons is over. Now the sovereignty of the individual – 'he/That wants himself is poor indeed' – is what counts. Lely's 1647 canvas portrays not a myth, but 'a Mind', the inner man that Civil War has made. A piece of psychological truth meets our eyes, the product of a new realism in art.

This interrogation of the imaginative process in an altered world, and that sense of the doubleness of things Lovelace acquired, are more than matched in Marvell. Janus, facing both ways, and Echo, hearing double, are the presiding deities of his verse: bifocalism and diplomatic devices ('secret meanings', 'allowed deceptions', 'shifting guiles') its habitual modes. Marvell's *An Horatian Ode* and *Tom Mays Death* (1650) make a typical diptych, posing alternatives – the first urging the ambitious poet to abandon verse, the second having him fight 'single' with the pen. Marvell never lacked courage or convictions; but he was given to secrecy and rightly apprehensive of being misunderstood, compounding differences. He never published either of these most public poems. Typically, he commits himself, but treads carefully. The next move looks like Carew's or Herrick's solution – the 'Rurall Sanctuary'. In fact the poems about Nun Appleton (where Fairfax lived in retirement) (1650–2), celebrating his well-earned recreation and the poet's appointment as the daughter's tutor, are full of warlike memories

Charles I with his second son James, as painted by Lely in 1648:
'a self-sufficient, loving, Christian stoic'.

and a sense of personal engagement. Marvell's patron was still, potentially, a power in the land. In his mind Marvell hears the Lord General's armour 'Rattling through the grove and hill'; closing his eyes he sees 'mountains rais'd of dying men'. Recollecting Eden,

> . . . that dear and happy isle
> The garden of the world ere while,
> Thou paradise of four seas,

he reflects that it was only mortal and has been laid 'waste'. Happily, Fairfax's gardens have not, like the gentleman's at Acton in 1643, been ripped up by vandalizing soldiers 'to the ruin of Art and Nature', though they *are* 'warlike', laid out in the 'figure of a fort'; and in the meadows – the image is sardonically posed – the mower's scythe sheds real blood, 'massacring' the harmless rail. Here, none the less, art and nature (non-idyllic) harmonize. What seemed to the poet's eye an unfathomable ocean becomes 'truly' that when the river floods it. Even 'the world . . . overthrown', the wasteland without, is accurately figured within, though micro-cosmically 'in more decent order tame'. Nun Appleton is a real place, not a dream. A fallen but redeemed landscape, it is now 'paradise's only map' to go by.

We no longer need the spectacular artifice of Inigo Jones' masques. Appleton's 'pleasant acts', masque-like turning-scenes, and *trompe l'oeil* perspective tricks are natural, and entertaining, revelations. *Upon Appleton House*, for all its playfulness,

*In 1650, Fairfax retired from soldiering and, in retreat at Nun
Appleton, inspired some of Marvell's finest poetry.*

is radically reformist both in the way it redeploys Jacobean and Caroline courtly
devices, and in its insistent millenarian perceptions. The place (emphatically
British Protestant), and the family, notably daughter Maria for whom there are
dynastic marriage plans, portend 'some universal good'. They, like Marvell, have
made 'destiny their choice'. Now with 'Lets in' we return to the house – another
seeming withdrawal but also (like Christ's return to His mother's house at the end
of *Paradise Regained*) a prelude to action. Within two years the poet had moved on:
first in 1653 to tutor Cromwell's ward (the matchless lyric *Bermudas*, celebrating
another natural paradise and Britain's missionary role, came of this); then with

Milton's help, to the Latin Secretaryship (1657); in the process emerging as the Protector's uncrowned laureate. Modest masques and other entertainments (Marvell's words among them, praising the Protector for replanting 'bays' in his old age) returned to Cromwell's court; and in Cromwellian achievements at home and overseas Marvell found something unequivocal to proclaim at large. In his *First Anniversary*, published in 1655, poetry recovered its place at the centre.

There were others, naturally, anxious to gravitate (or is it levitate?) there in pursuit of patronage and the power to make things happen. Lovelace's friend, John Hall of Durham, in 1647 had quit the 'sullen groves' of Cavalier verse to serve the 'Public Interest' in other literary ways. And eventually even non-Republicans like D'Avenant, Cowley and Waller, all Paris exiles from 1646–50, drifted home by various routes to make their peace with Cromwell. D'Avenant, last laureate to Charles I tried, even under sentence of death in Carisbrooke Castle in 1650, to keep the office going with *Gondibert*, an heroic romance. Friends, notably Hobbes, whose celebrated correspondence with D'Avenant was published before the poem, endorsed the heroic mode and realistic neo-classicism. The cool style, with fancy well under judgement's thumb, the commonsense air, and the dismissal of gods and goddesses along with all kinds of spoofs and enchantments, appealed to the *literati*. Here were 'Men and Manners' as they knew them. Others laughed at the poet's pretensions. They wanted action and military heroes, not pale, passive ciphers. Unfortunately one Englishman's hero was now another's villain; and you could hardly, as Cowley earlier confessed, offer laurels to the conquered. *Gondibert* (1651) was a brave attempt to get round that dilemma by celebrating patient virtue. It remained unfinished. In due course D'Avenant emerged from the Tower to play, enemies alleged, 'Master of the Revels' to Oliver. He certainly wrote and produced plays acceptable to the Protector, and introduced opera to England. The laureateship of the market had arrived.

Cowley, meanwhile, tried another tack. Making literature sound like one of the ruins Cromwell knocked about a bit (which it wasn't) he offered in 1656 to 'dismantle . . . all the works and fortifications of wit' of unregenerate days – his volume of anaemic love-lyrics *The Mistress* (1647), doubtless among them. Discovering the Protector was not a philistine, he set about some large-scale renovation instead. The Pindaric Ode made its début. And *Davideis* (1656), the first neo-classical religious epic in English was launched: 'I sing the man who Judah's sceptre bore'. It was a daunting task and with only four of twelve books ever completed, another honourable failure. This time the problem was not lack of heroes. David and the Israelites effectively shadow Cromwell and the New Model Army; but Cowley, who elsewhere lauded Cromwell as a modern Brutus, is here discreet to a fault. He cannot bring himself to be more than half-hearted about the story's messianic, prophetic message or respond positively to the Biblical history of civil disorder and power struggles. Essentially he abhors such things and takes refuge in Hobbist maxims and politically neutral moral stoicism. There are effective passages, notably scenes recycled from *The Civil War*. He catches something of the scale and epoch-making significance of Britain's upheavals and he did put Virgilian ambition centre-stage. One understands Milton esteeming him. But Cowley, harping on about the 'happy Isle . . . how chang'd and curst', was never wholly in or out of tune with Cromwellian times.

To amiable Edmund Waller, untroubled by Cowley's lingering resentments, everything seemed straightforward. By land and sea Cromwell's writ ran: no one could say now, as in the 1630s, that the English were 'effeminate, incapable of discipline, absented from warlike employments'. In the new 'glorious state', once more at peace with itself but formidable abroad, heroic-song – proper accompaniment of empire – will find its voice. The muses' whereabouts are no longer a problem: 'every Conqueror creates' one. Cromwell, commanding the arts of peace and war (for he repaired his country too) is truly the great Augustus that Charles I failed to be. Waller sees the opportunity and talks of illustrious deeds infusing 'high raptures'. Significantly he does not intend the old kind of visionary flight. With D'Avenant, Hobbes and the rest, he thought the 'rage' of Civil War and the nonsensical rhapsodies of zealots had discredited the *furor poeticus*. Inspiration was suspect. But the heroic measure of things, which civil conflict challenged and frustrated, had been made good by the Protectorate's acts. No *Cromwelliad*, however, was ever written. For when he died British history soon painted him the villain of the piece. Marvell, had the Protector lived, might have done it. At least, he grasped the epic scope of his achievements – the irresistible force with which he had shattered the old mould and cast the Kingdom anew, the magnanimity and skill of his rebuilding to transform 'the resistance of opposed minds' into a united front. His Cromwell may be a messianic leader, but he is no magus or demi-god. 'The man' – Marvell insists on the term – is, all confess, a great soldier and statesman, a charismatic figure shaping history under providence. No longer trapped in ritual politics, we enter a subtly transformed and more familiar world. Not the old order, and not the Utopia some had fought for; but built on a grand scale to last. The Protector's Civil Service, full of men of ability and learning, his administrative and taxation system (a product of armies' and navies' needs) and his foreign policies would survive. Efficient stable government and keep-your-powder-dry pragmatism were among Cromwell's great bequests to the nation he loved. He would hardly have thrilled when Waller's post-Restoration muse found 'tea' sufficient inspiration! Milton, luckily, still had other ideas. It was a relief to polite society, none the less, not to feel the ground move underfoot any more. The muses, more metropolitan now and self-assured, had moved into their mansions.

IV

Satire, the other side of the heroic coin, was at home as never before. Turn that coin, and Cromwell changes from Augustus to overweening Phaeton comically thrown from his carriage in Hyde Park – an ominous come-uppance. All-conquering Oliver is only old copper-nosed Nol after all. So Prince Rupert, earlier, is rudely exposed as owner of an obscene she-monkey and a dog in cahoots with Lucifer. Not subtle stuff! But sometimes crudely, sometimes with urbane aplomb, in satire, burlesque, caricature, parody, travesty, mock-heroic, and all the forms (pornography included) of literary merry-making, the daemons of the day were set loose and exorcized. There is no place in such literature of laughter for languishing, or self-doubt, or the Civil War within. Doubleness and division still prevail, but firmly externalized and made over into the other side's diabolical (literally 'two-tongued') duplicity:

So 'twixt their double madness here's the odds,
One makes false Devills, t'other makes false Gods.

The norm is here defined not by courtly sanction and taste, but the mean between extremes, the commonsense antithesis of madnesses. So Cowley deploys the couplet's inherent qualities of balance and opposition to point and contain excess, and instil the virtues of straightforwardness and singleness of mind, just as Dryden would in

Gods they had tried of every shape and size
That God-smiths could produce, or Priests devize

The very things that bedevilled laureate endeavour, aided and abetted satire. Significantly, when Cowley's *Civil War* loses pitch under pressure of events, it drifts down into elegy and satire, mourning and castigating. Partisan tearfulness and angry rebuttal – neither of which needs victory – proliferate in 1640s propaganda, defining difference while concensus disintegrates. Cowley's pioneering *The Puritan and the Papist* (1643) established the oppositional paradigm. In a rapidly politicized society, polarization prevailed. Do satirists, castigating difference, also compound it? Discord and fragmentation, the collapse of unanimity and conformity, the distortion of language were certainly grist to their mill. So dissenting preachers' way with text ('dividing' and expounding it phrase by phrase) becomes butchering it 'into many dead parts breaking the sense and words all to pieces' – a penetrating image of the injury done to meaning and the body politic by division. But where would laughter be without it?

John Cleveland's *Rebel Scot*, to innoculate against infection, sarcastically revels in the prospect of a nation 'sicke of Pym's disease' – John Pym got the Northerners to invade in 1643. Panegyric is out, but back-handed compliments work perfectly:

Had Cain been Scot, God would have changed his doom,
Not forced him wander, but confined him home.

He did not; and now it is 'as if the devil had ubiquity'. Cleveland's ironic Biblical exegesis, apocalyptic innuendo and parodic inversions, which became a feature of both sides' propaganda, simultaneously (such is satire's latent ambiguity) flourished and subverted hypocrisy. There was a bit of 'devil' in Cleveland too, sending himself up in witty burlesque of 'Metaphysical' paradoxes or deflating the foe with unkind colloquialism. 'What a godly thing is want of shirts', mocking Scottish poverty, put Presbyterianism in its place. So Cleveland's juxtapositions and deliberate disjunctions – very different from Cowley's lofty, smooth classical Augustanism – recreated and criticized the cacophony of competing voices.

The brickbats flew, thick and fast. Englishmen may not have relished killing one another in earnest, but verbal mayhem was another matter, and emphatically marketable. Suddenly slander – abominated in the old honorific society – paid handsomely; and verbal wounding was legitimate. Satiric verse, prose, and drama (in the form of play pamphlets) had a field day. The boundaries between élite and popular literature were blurred and crossed. Court and University wits (like Berkenhead, Cowley, Cleveland for the Court; Nedham and Hall of Durham for Parliament) moved into journalism. Hacks made a play for more sophisticated readers. Colloquialism, the language of the street, so to speak, passed into polite letters: classical references, rhetorical devices, and learned touches infiltrated popular verse. Nor was satire confined any longer to castigating general types. Stereotyping still features – Rebel and Malignant, Puritan and Papist, Roundhead and Cavalier. But the targeting of specific contemporaries increasingly predominates. Here Laud and Strafford, there Pym, Hampden, Marten are pilloried. Things topical, documentary, robustly personal are never far away. Satire gleefully unmasks (a favourite figure) the individual hidden behind the ikon.

When tradesmen and apprentices played at politics, unlettered preachers spoke from pulpits, and unlanded *arrivistes* acquired other men's estates, satire found rich pickings. Women, too, stepped out of line. *A Spirit Moving in the Women Preachers* earnestly denounces the 'strange new Feminine Brood'. War produced new liberties. The Countess of Derby put on the breeches to command the garrison at Lathom House, becoming a heroine in Cavalier eyes, a comic harridan in London newsbooks. At Lyme Regis the townswomen under Royalist siege helped actively in defence, carrying powder, charging muskets, and hurling stones at men scaling the walls. James Strong's *Joanerides: or Feminine Valour* (1645) attempts Homeric, Virgilian flights in their praise; but it is prefaced by platoons of verses mocking the country bumpkin author and the women's heroism. In 1642 for the first time in British history women petitioned Parliament: they were swiftly and bawdily ('each of us', they protest, 'had as loving and kinde husband as ever laid leg over woman') put in their place by a mock-petition. The Mistress Parliament pamphlet plays of the late 1640s – such things kept drama in play though theatres were closed – were similarly, though more inventively hostile to female activism. In this world-turned-upside-down and back-to-front the language of topsy-turveydom prevailed: when the House of Lords was abolished in 1649, the Earl of Pembroke was made to boast of his 'ascent downwards' to the Commons. Spoof speeches, sermons, last wills and testaments – sometimes not easily detected – wrung humour from the confusion of categories.

The laughter got louder, more raucous, in the Interregnum. Debunking was in the air. Natural deism and Hobbist materialism (who else would liken an inspired poet to a pair of bagpipes!) found their way into popular verse. The percentage of religious verse fell. Samuel Butler's *Hudibras* (1663) retrospectively summed up the mood, pillorying all forms of enthusiasm, and Utopianism, all occult and hermetic adumbrations, all astrologers and alchemists, and the whole apparatus of Arthurian-Spenserian romance. The great and traumatic struggle over religion and liberty was reduced to 'Apostolick blows and knocks', and ridiculed in jog-trot rhythms and farcical rhymes:

> When pulpit, drum ecclesiastick
> Was beat with fist, instead of a stick

Meanwhile in the 1650s, volumes like *Sportive Wit, Choyce Drollery, Wit and Drollery*, with sophisticates like Sir John Denham, Cleveland, Berkenhead, James Smith and Sir John Mennis pitching in, laughed solemnity to scorn. Nothing was sacred, not even Homer and Virgil, let alone Cavalier fashions: 'the pitifull whining passion of Love', idyllic pastoral, and heroic hyperbole are

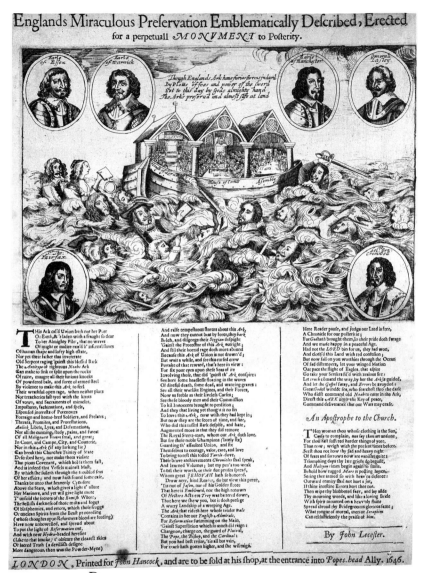

Parliamentary propaganda (in word and visual image) was iconoclastic but not iconophobic.

derided along with prigs, Puritans, and assorted grotesques. These Drolleries go back a long way pre-war, but the mode was especially popular in the Cavalier literary 'clubs' of the 1640s. John Taylor's *Mad Verse, Sad Verse, Glad Verse, and Bad Verse* (1644) sum it up succinctly:

> I weeping sing the maddest mad Rebellion
> That ever Story told, or Tongue can tell you on.

137

Later drolleries (often rehearsing earlier material as Moseley's politer volumes do) left sad verse behind. Cheerful stoicism, conviviality and ribaldry were the thing, offering escape and resistance to 'the violent assaults of Melancholy assisted by the additionall Engines and Weapons of Sack and good Company'. Manifestly the memory of war and defeat lingers, but these men will have the last laugh in their cups and 'good verses'. 'Since all the world is mad' their mockery stands for sanity. Raffishness and playful rudery were nothing new; but the general tone is coarser than pre-war, more scurrilous, lecherous and hard-boiled. More lavatorial too, sometimes, than we expect of Cromwellian times, as when Mennis commemorated heroic feats of defecation to send up the classics and shock the sensitive. The drolleries catered for a broader, more cynical, though not unsophisticated audience than of old. The wits follow the market: 'it must be Drolleries or it will not please'. The coin they dealt in – heroism its other face – paid tribute to the gods of realism. Levity and gravity alike honour critical rationalism and common sense. The currency of fashionable literature now was not 'rage Poetick' but 'Men and Manners', high and low. Visionary and dissenting discourses did not disappear; but the controlling mood of the nation, that is to say of its capital city, had come round, you could say righted itself, well before the Merry Monarch returned to claim his own.

V

Once more the agenda changed. Visionary politics were laughed off-stage, perhaps for good. As Milton observed, laughter and anger are the 'two most rational faculties of the human soul'; and rationalism, in Hobbist, Butlerian, and drolling shapes swept to victory. The new rationalists did not, however, have a monopoly of amusement. Milton's own satiric wit and crude boisterous humour are evident from undergraduate days: low 'Billingsgate' language was part of his armoury. He would mock, scoff, jeer and taunt with the best of them. There is no line more scathing than 'New Presbyter is but Old Priest writ large'; no more insultingly personal ridicule than his of Charles I in *Eikonoklastes* (1649). That the Rabelaisian *Wit and Drollery* and *Sportive Wit* (including '*à la mode* Lampoons on some Heroic Persons of these Late Times') were edited by his nephew John Phillips (who was also his pupil and amanuensis), seems odd until we recollect the gross scurrility and gleeful sexual innuendo of Milton's demolition of Salmasius in 1650. He may well have been behind Phillips's penchant for satire and coarse language. *Paradise Lost* (1667) is hardly the place for drollery or Billingsgate. But a vein of satiric irony and sardonic humour runs through the epic. Its vision of married love is counterpointed by dismissal of the harlots 'bought smile':

> Casual Fruition . . . Court Amours,
> Mixt Dance, or wanton Mask, or Midnight Ball
> Or Serenate, which the starved lover sings
> To his proud fair.

There is a lofty contempt in that. Satan's scoffing, Christ's rebuttals of Satanic temptations in *Paradise Regained*, or Samson's of Harapha and Delila in *Samson Agonistes* – all have the same ring. 20 years of fearless, often highly personalized controversy (for he rightly believed there is no separating the point of view from the person expressing it) went to the making of these things.

There is recent history, too, in his epic's wars. The chariots, spears, helmets, shields are Biblical and Classical but 'ensanguin'd Fields scattered . . . with Carcases', 'where Cattel pastured late' are more like Wither methodized. Even the angelic aerial battle has its coincidental analogue in spectral armies in the sky seen fighting it out again after Edgehill. More tangibly, the heavenly host in 'mighty Quadrate joynd/Of union irresistible', advancing in the cause 'Of God and his Messiah' recall the New Model Army in close phalanx, locked together, riding knee to knee. And angels apart, the sad irony

> . . . that Angel shall with Angel Warr
> And in fierce hosting meet who wont to meet
> So oft in Festivals of joy and love
> Unanimous

sums up lamentations for halcyon days.

Milton's, indeed, is the last and loveliest of Caroline Arcadias, noblest of Caroline love scenes, and most richly sensuous and poignant evocation of Love and Beauty, not as cult but part of our common humanity:

> So hand in hand they passed, the loveliest pair
> That ever since in loves imbraces met.

The machinations that destroy all that, were things Milton had lived through. The final going forward, too, with 'Providence their guide' echoes Milton's earlier vision of the British people 'in the wilderness . . . though under God's immediate government'. His sense of being isolated, an internal exile in evil days, and the uncertain immediate outlook at the Restoration are caught in the 'wandering steps and slow' and 'solitarie way' – *Paradise Lost*'s last words. Milton knew what defeat felt like (there were none in England now who did not know) and that there was no going back. The old dispensation is done for: modern history lies ahead. Human individuals, responsible for their actions, must 'choose'. *Paradise Lost* is not, crudely, about the Civil War and what ensued; but that experience is embedded in Milton's tragi-heroic vision of the human lot.

He forged an idiom, unlike any other, capable, by virtue of its large and subtle movement, of tracing the loss and recovery of wholeness through the twists and turns of destiny. The age's many literary modes, from lyric to epic, from Cavalier to Puritan, went to its making. All the time's contending forces are felt as the poem patterns divergences and differences, oppositions, contradictions, confusions and cross-purposes, the loss of unanimity in division and self-division and the grand underlying drive towards restoring lost integrity. All the exhilaration and guilt, all the immense destructive and creative energies of the century are gathered up and released, transformed, in the poem's 'fearful symmetry'.

Milton took, as Marvell noted, enormous risks. How perilously close the 'nightly visitation' of his Celestial Patroness's inspiration comes to Satan's fly-by-night temptations, whispering insidious dreams in Eve's ear. How close 'The Mind is its own place' (a piece of Cavalier stoicism!) seems to Milton's own indomitable pursuit of 'higher Argument', especially since it might 'be mine/Not Hers who brings it nightly to my ear'. No one, not even Marvell,

Milton on Cromwell

When war broke out, he offered his services and was put in command of a squadron of horse, but because of the concourse of good men who flocked to his standards from all sides, his force was greatly increased and he soon surpassed well-nigh the greatest generals both in the magnitude of his accomplishments and in the speed with which he achieved them. Nor was this remarkable, for he was a soldier well-versed in self-knowledge, and whatever enemy lay within – vain hopes, fear, desires – he had either previously destroyed within himself or had long since reduced to subjection. Commander first over himself, victor over himself, he had learned to achieve over himself the most effective triumph, and so, on the very first day that he took service against an external foe, he entered camp a veteran and past-master in all that concerned the soldier's life . . . May you then, O Cromwell, increase in your magnanimity, for it becomes you. You, the liberator of your country, the author of liberty, and likewise its guardian and saviour, can undertake no more distinguished role and none more august. By your deeds you have outstripped not only the achievements of our kings, but even the legends of our heroes . . . You have taken upon yourself by far the heaviest burden, one that will put to the test your inmost capacities, that will search you out wholly and intimately, and reveal what spirit, what strength, what authority are in you, whether there truly live in you that piety, faith, justice, and moderation of soul which convince us that you have been raised by the power of God beyond all other men to this most exalted rank. To rule with wisdom three powerful nations, to desire to lead their peoples from base customs to a better standard of morality and discipline than before, to direct your solicitous mind and thoughts into the most distant regions, to be vigilant, to exercise foresight, to refuse no toil, to yield to no allurements of pleasure, to flee from the pomp of wealth and power, these are arduous tasks compared to which war is a mere game.

*Extract from Milton's *A Second Defence of the English People*, 30 May 1654 (in *complete Prose works vol IV, 1650–55* ed. Don M. Wolf, Yale University Press, 1966).

subjected art and imagination to such deep and daring scrutiny. Against the grain of fashion, the poet insists, perforce, on Christian inspiration, for that alone separates true from false prophets and redeems human energies (poetry included) from self-destructiveness. He knows 'if all be mine' will not do. Nor will man-made rhyme, though all the rage in town. He liberates himself, therefore, from that 'troublesome and modern bondage' with its petty constraints and jingling harmonies, not just to follow Homer and Virgil but that his muse might be free to inspire his 'unpremeditated verse'. So Milton looked, as his heirs the Romantics would, beyond the rules of art.

The polished heroic couplet and its uses swept the board. It represents a central and characteristic achievement of the century. But it was not the

Authors Referred to in the Text

Bastwick, Dr John	1593–1654	Divine and pamphleteer
Berkenhead, Sir John	1617–79	Royalist journalist
Booker, John	1603–67	Astrologer
Butler, Samuel	1612–80	Poet
Carew, Thomas	1612–80	Cavalier poet
Cleveland, John	1613–58	Royalist poet and propagandist
Cowley, Abraham	1618–87	Poet
Daniel, George	1616–57	Cavalier Poet
Daniel, Samuel	1563–1619	Poet
D'Avenant, Sir William	1606–68	Poet and playwright
Dell, William	1607?–70	Reformist scholar and divine
Denham, Sir John	1615–69	Royalist poet
Dryden, John	1631–1700	Poet
Hall, John of Durham	1627–56	Poet and Republican propagandist
Herrick, Robert	1591–1674	Cavalier poet
Hobbes, Thomas	1588–1679	Philosopher
Lilly, William	1602–81	Astrologer
Lovelace, Richard	1618–57	Cavalier poet
Marten, Henry	1602–80	MP and Regicide
Marvell, Andrew	1621–78	Poet and politician
Mennis, Sir John	1599–1671	Poet and admiral
Milton, John	1608–74	Poet and pamphleteer
Nedham, Marchmont	1620–78	Journalist
Peter, Hugh	1598–1660	Independent divine
Quarles, John	1624–65	Poet
Salmasius, Claudius	1588–1653	French divine
Sidney, Sir Philip	1554–86	Poet, soldier, statesman
Smith, Dr James	1605–67	Poet and divine
Strong, James	fl. 1645	Poet and divine
Taylor, Jeremy	1613?–1667	Divine
Taylor, John	1578–1653	Poet-journalist
Thomason, George	d. 1666	Bookseller
Vaughan, Henry	1621–95	Poet
Waller, Edmund	1606–87	Poet
Wharton, Sir George	1617–81	Astrologer
Wither, George	1588–1667	Poet

sum of things. Marvell, 'transported by the mode' like all the others, knew it was a lesser vehicle, not up to Milton's sustained flight. In him an old English tradition (blank verse) and Puritan apocalyptic and confessional modes triumphed against the odds. Paradoxically, that 'ancient liberty recover'd to Heroic poem' is used to subvert conventional heroism, breaking the ancient epic bond with war. Not that it is ever far away: but the blind seer's eye is fixed on something loftier than 'Warre, hithertoo the only Argument/Heroic deem'd'. So he faces and frees himself from defeat. Not 'Arms and the Man' any more; but 'Of Man's first disobedience . . . till one greater Man/Restore us'. Epic's proper theme, like life's purpose, is self-conquest, strength won from weakness, and humble acknowledgement of God's providence. We are directed towards the better (post-lapsarian) Paradise Within not as an escape from the fallen world but to prepare for action in it. *Paradise Lost* was – and is – a revolutionary poem designed to make things happen.

Even political opponents – for Milton's epic is not narrowly partisan or merely topical – stood astonished. 'The noblest poem', proclaimed Sir John Denham, sheets hot from the press in his hand, 'that ever was wrote in any language or in any age'. No mean tribute from Royalist to regicide. Only Dryden put it better: 'This man cuts us all out, and the ancients too'. It was a mighty coming of age. The continuities of seventeenth-century life and literature are undeniable; but there is no mistaking the new expression – not altogether comfortable – on the face of things. Many forces went to its making, and there were losses as well as gains along the way. War, nevertheless, that great engine of change, had left a deep and lasting mark on Britain, without breaking it. In many ways, indeed, the nation and its literature emerged not just more or less intact, but braced and modernized by the experience: tougher, more diverse, more ambitious and more dynamic than before.

In 1917 Joseph Conrad, in *The Shadow-Line*, a sea story, paid tribute obliquely, and without idealizing war, to his son's generation fighting and dying in the trenches. It is a tale of immaturity tested and tempered by adversity, evil and self-doubt. The young hero comes through, as Cromwell did in Milton's estimation, because he first overcame his enemies within. So seventeenth-century Britain, passing through the storm of a warlike, various and tragical age, crossed *its* shadow-line.

Further Reading

Introduction

For general background to the themes of this introduction and this book, the following are but a representative sample from the legion of available works:

Derek Hirst, *Authority and Conflict 1603–1658* (1986).

Lawrence Stone, *The Causes of the English Revolution* (1972).

Conrad Russell, *The Causes of the English Civil War* (1990).

Anthony Fletcher, *The Outbreak of the English Civil War* (1979).

John Morrill, *The Revolt of the Provinces* (1980).

John Kenyon, *The Civil Wars in England* (1987).

John Kenyon, *The Stuart Constitution* (2nd edn, 1986).

David Underdown, *Revel, Riot and Rebellion* (1985).

Frank MacGregor and Barry Reay (eds.), *Radical Religion in the English Revolution* (1982).

John Morrill (ed.), *Reactions to the English Civil War* (1982).

CHAPTER I
The Impact of the Fighting

There is no shortage of excellent books on the Civil Wars. J. P. Kenyon's *The Civil Wars of England* (London, 1988), is the best recent survey that combines military and political history. *The English Civil Wars: a military History of the three Civil Wars, 1642–51* (1974) by Peter Young and Richard Holmes is an excellent introduction. Austin Woolrych's *Battles of the English Civil War* (1961), and A. H. Burne's *The Battlefields of England* (1951) deal with the confrontations between armies, while individual battles are covered by the many books and articles by the doyen of Civil War historians, Brigadier Peter Young. John Adair, *By the Sword Divided, Eyewitness accounts of the English Civil War* (London, 1983) and Richard Ollard, *This War without an Enemy: a history of the English Civil War* (1976), are good short accounts.

Regional studies, such as Clive Holmes's *The Eastern Association during the English Civil War* (Cambridge, 1974), John Morrill's *The Revolt of the Provinces* (1976), and David Stevenson's *The Scottish Revolution, 1637–44* (Newton Abbot, 1973), are useful. C. H. Firth, *Cromwell's Army* (1962), and C. H. Firth and G. Davies, *The Regimental History of Cromwell's Armies* (2 vols., Oxford, 1940) are fundamental for the Roundheads, while Mark Kishlansky's *The Rise of the New Model Army* (Cambridge, 1979) is a provocative interpretation. For the Cavaliers, Ronald Hutton, *The Royalist War Effort, 1642–46* (1983), is valuable, while Joyce Malcolm, *Caesar's Due: Loyalty and King Charles, 1642–1646* (1983), should be used for its data rather than for its conclusions.

In the last few years, as part of the growing interest in Civil War re-enactments and war gaming, Partizan Press has started an ambitious programme of producing new editions of military memoirs as well as reasonably priced photocopies of contemporary pamphlets. A current catalogue may be obtained by writing to Partizan Press, 26 Cliffsea Grove, Leigh-on-Sea, SS9 1NQ.

Of the eight hundred or so contemporary descriptions of the Civil Wars the following are among the most interesting and available:

E. Archer, *A True Relation of the Red Trained Bands of Westminster, the Green Auxiliaries of London and the Yellow Auxiliaries of the Tower Hamlets . . . 16 October to 20 December 1643* (London, 1643).

J. A. Atkinson, *Tracts relating to the civil war in Cheshire, 1641–59* (Chetham Society, 1909).

Richard Atkyns, *Vindication of Richard Atkyns* (1669, edited by P. Young and N. Tucker, 1967).

Richard Baxter, *Reliquiae Baxterianae, or . . . Baxter's narrative of the most memorable passages of his life* (1696, later editions).

Colonel John Birch, *Military Memoirs* (Camden Society, 1873).

Sir Richard Bulstrode, *Memoirs* (London, 1721).

Robert Douglas, 'Civil War Diary', in James Madiment, ed., *Historical Fragments Relating to Scottish Affairs* (Edinburgh, 1832).

Sergeant Henry Foster, *A True and Exact Relation of the marchings of the trained bands of the City of London . . . To the Relief of Gloucester* (1643, reprinted Gloucester, 1828, and Leigh-on-Sea, 1990).

Captain John Gwynn, *Military Memoirs* (Edinburgh 1822, and Kineton, 1967).

Captain J. Hodgson, *Memoirs* (Bradford, 1902).

Sir Ralph Hopton, *Bellum Civile: Sir Ralph Hopton's Memoirs of the Campaign in the West, 1642–1644* edited by C. E. H. Chadwyck Healey (Somerset Record Society, 1902), and by Alan Wicks (Leigh-on-Sea, 1988).

Lucy Hutchinson, *Memoirs of the Life of Colonel Hutchinson* (1973).

Edmund Ludlow, *Memoirs* (Oxford, 1894).

Henry Townsend, *Diary* (Worcester Historical Society, 1920).

Chaplain Joshua Sprigge, *Anglia Rediviva . . . Being the History of the army . . . Under Sir Thomas Fairfax (1647, 1854).*

Captain Richard Symmonds, *Diary of the Marches of the Royal Army during the Great Civil War* (Camden Society, 1859 and Leigh-on-Sea, 1990).

Nehemiah Wharton, 'The Letters of Nehemiah Wharton,' ed., Sir Henry Ellis, *Archaeologia*, XXV (1853), S. L. Ede-Borrett (Leigh-on-Sea, 1983).

CHAPTER II
The Impact on Government

The most helpful introductions to the history of English government during the 1640s are G. E. Aylmer, *Rebellion or Revolution? England 1640–1660* (Oxford, 1986); and Derek Hirst, *Authority and Conflict: England 1603–1658* (London, 1986).

The fullest political narrative, with excellent analyses of all the main constitutional measures, remains that presented in S. R. Gardiner, *History of England from the accession of James I to the outbreak of the Civil War, 1603–1642* (10 vols., London, 1883–4), vol. X; and *History of the Great Civil War, 1642–1649* (4 vols., London, 1893). For the period 1640–2, Anthony Fletcher, *The Outbreak of the English Civil War* (London, 1981) is also very useful.

The administrative reforms of the Civil War years, and their impact on provincial government, are discussed in John Morrill, *The Revolt of the Provinces: Conservatives and Radicals in the English Civil War, 1630–1650* (Longman edition, London, 1980); and in *Reactions to the English Civil War, 1642–1649*, ed. John Morrill (London, 1982).

The role of the nobility in government is examined in J. S. A. Adamson, 'The English Nobility and the Projected Settlement of 1647', *Historical Journal*, XXX (1987), 567–602; and 'The Baronial Context of the English Civil War', *Transactions of the Royal Historical Society*, 5th series, XL (1990), 93–120.

Jonathan Scott, 'Radicalism and Restoration: The Shape of the Stuart Experience', *Historical Journal*, XXXI (1988), 453–67, gives an interesting overview of seventeenth-century constitutional developments.

Finally, throughout this essay I have quoted extensively from two fundamental collections of documents: *The Constitutional Documents of the Puritan Revolution, 1625–1660*, ed. S. R. Gardiner (3rd edition, Oxford, 1906); and *The Stuart Constitution*, ed. J. P. Kenyon (2nd edition, Cambridge, 1986). The latter also contains a very important and illuminating commentary.

CHAPTER III
The Impact of Puritanism

The best introduction to the religious background to the Civil Wars is now Conrad Russell, *The Causes of the English Civil War* (Oxford, 1990), published just as this book went to press. John Morrill, 'The Religious Context of the English Civil War', *Trans. Royal Hist. Soc.,* 5th ser. vol. 34 (1984), 'The Attack on the Church of England in the Long Parliament' in eds. D. Beales and G. Best, *History, Society and the Churches* (Cambridge, 1985) and 'Sir William Brereton and England's "Wars of Religion"', *Jnl of Brit. Studs.*, xxiv (1985), explore the themes of this essay in greater depth. A. Fletcher, *The Outbreak of the English Civil War* (1981) is especially strong on religious issues at Westminster and in the provinces, while William Hunt, *The Puritan Moment* (Cambridge, Mass., 1983), is a case study of the explosion of pent-up religious energy in one county (Essex).

W. A. Shaw, *A History of the English Church during the Civil Wars and under the Commonwealth* (2 vols., 1900), is as long, detailed and unimaginative as its title suggests; but it is a mine of useful information. George Yule, *Puritans and Politics* (Sutton Courtney, 1981) is an account of the disputes about Church government in the mid-1640s in the Long Parliament; while Robert Paul, *The Assembly of the Lord* (Edinburgh, 1985) offers an exhaustive (exhausting!) account of the Westminster Assembly that superseded all previous ones. Robert Paul, *The Apologeticall Narration* (1961) consists of a facsimile printing of the tract with an invaluable essay.

Anglican survivalism is discussed by John Morrill, 'The Church in England, 1642–9' in ed. John Morrill, *Reactions to the English Civil War* (1982), and the iconoclasm in M. Aston, *England's Iconoclasts* (Oxford, 1988).

William Haller, *Liberty and Reformation in the Puritan Revolution* (New York, 1955) is the classic account of religious writings in the 1640s; but it must be supplemented by William Lamont, *Godly Rule* (1970) a series of suggestive essays on the millenarian itch in seventeenth-century divinity. It is supplemented by an important essay by Lamont in eds. R. C. Richardson and G. M. Ridden, *Freedom and the English Revolution* (Manchester, 1986).

J. F. Macgregor and B. Reay, *Radical Religion in the English Civil War* (Oxford, 1984) is a generally stimulating set of essays about the sects; and Christopher Hill's *The World Turned Upside Down* (Harmondsworth, 1972) is a classic account of their thoughts and actions. G. Nuttall *Visible Saints* (Oxford, 1957) writing from within the tradition, offers the best introductory guide to the Congregationalists. J. C. Davis's *Fear, Myth and History* (Cambridge, 1986), a study of the Ranter phenomenon, is a refreshing counsel of caution against getting the sects out of context and out of proportion; while his essay on 'The Levellers and Christianity' in ed. B. S. Manning, *Politics, Religion and the English Civil War* (Manchester, 1973) remains the best introduction.

No study of the religious developments of this period can afford to leave Oliver Cromwell out of account. The biography which brings out his religious preoccupations best is probably R. S. Paul, *The Lord Protector* (1955); but it is a central theme of most of the essays in ed. J. S. Morrill, *Oliver Cromwell and the English Revolution* (1990).

CHAPTER IV
The Impact on Political Thought

The most useful introductions to political thought in the 1640s are:

John Sanderson, *'But the People's Creatures': The Philosophical Basis of the English Civil War* (Manchester, 1989).

Andrew Sharp, *Political Ideas of the English Civil Wars 1641–1649* (London, 1983).

J. P. Sommerville, 'Oliver Cromwell and English Political Thought', in J. S. Morrill (ed.), *Oliver Cromwell and the English Revolution* (London, 1990).

Austin Woolrych, 'Political Theory and Political Practice', in C. A. Patrides and R. B. Waddington (eds.), *The Age of Milton: Backgrounds to Seventeenth-Century Literature* (Manchester, 1980).

David Wootton, *Divine Right and Democracy: An Anthology of Political Writing in Stuart England* (Harmondsworth, 1986).

Perez Zagorin, *A History of Political Thought in the English Revolution* (London, 1954).

CHAPTER V
The Impact of the New Model Army

C. H. Firth, *Cromwell's Army* (4th edn., 1962).

C. H. Firth and G. Davies, *A Regimental History of Cromwell's Army* (2 vols., 1940).

I. Gentles, *The New Model Army in England, Ireland and Scotland, 1645–1653* (1991).

M. A. Kishlansky, *The Rise of the New Model Army* (1979).

A. Woolrych, *Soldiers and Statesmen: The General Council of the Army and its debates, 1647–1648* (1987).

J. S. A. Adamson, 'The English Nobility and the Projected Settlement of 1647', *Historical Journal* 30 (1987).

P. Crawford, '"Charles Stuart, that Man of Blood"', *Journal of British Studies* 16 (1977).

I. Gentles, 'Arrears of pay and ideology in the Army Revolt of 1647', *War and Society*, 1 (1977).

I. Gentles, 'The struggle for London in the second civil war', *Historical Journal* 26 (1983).

M. A. Kishlansky, 'What Happened at Ware?' *Historical Journal* 25 (1982).

M. A. Kishlansky, 'Ideology and Politics in the Parliamentary Armies, 1645–9', in ed. J. Morrill, *Reactions to the English Civil War* (1982).

J. S. Morrill, 'Mutiny and Discontent in English Provincial Armies' *Past and Present* 56 (1972).

J. S. Morrill, 'The Army Revolt of 1647', in eds. A. Duke and C. Tamse, *Britain and the Netherlands*, 6 (1978).

A. Woolrych, 'Cromwell as a soldier' in ed. J. Morrill, *Oliver Cromwell and the English Revolution* (1990).

CHAPTER VI
The Impact on Society

On the social structure of seventeenth-century England, there are two good social histories which also offer background discussion to many of the themes raised in this chapter:

Keith Wrightson, *English Society 1580–1680* (1982).

J. A. Sharpe, *Early Modern England: A Social History 1550–1760* (1987).

On the centrality of the family to the ideology of order and challenges to domestic and gender relations:

Susan Amussen, *An Ordered Society: Gender and Class in early Modern England* (Oxford, 1988).

C. Durston, *The Family in the English Revolution* (Oxford, 1989).

On the challenge of the sects and radicals:

C. Hill, *The World Turned Upside Down: Radical Ideas during the English Revolution* (1972), a magisterial study which perhaps tends to conflate the radical with the popular.

J. F. McGregor and B. Reay (eds.), *Radical Religion in the English Revolution* (Oxford, 1984).

K. Thomas, 'Women in the Civil War Sects', in T. Aston (ed.), *Crisis in Europe, 1560–1660* (1965).

P. Mack, 'The Prophet and Her Audience: Gender and Knowledge in the World Turned Upside Down' in G. Eley and W. Hunt (eds.), *Reviving the English Revolution* (1988).

D. P. Ludlow, 'Shaking Patriarchy's Foundations: Sectarian Women in England

1641–1700', in R. L. Greaves (ed.), *Triumph over Silence: Women in Protestant History* (1985).

On Puritan attempts to reform popular culture:
David Underdown, *Revel, Riot and Rebellion: Popular Politics and Culture in England 1603–1660* (Oxford, 1985).
K. Thomas, 'The Puritans and Adultery: the Act of 1650 Reconsidered' in D. Pennington and K. Thomas (eds.), *Puritans and Revolutionaries* (Oxford, 1978).

On collective disorder in the 1640s:
A. Charlesworth (ed.), *An Atlas of Rural Protest in Britain 1549–1900* (1983).
K. Lindley, 'London and popular freedom in the 1640s' in R. C. Richardson and G. M. Ridden (eds.), *Freedom and the English revolution: Essays in History and Literature* (Manchester, 1986).
W. Hunt, *The Puritan Moment: The Coming of Revolution in an English County* (1983).
B. Manning, *The English People and the English Revolution* (1976), a book which argues convincingly for the importance of the people in influencing the events of the Revolution.
    Both Manning and Hunt, however, should be read in conjunction with:
J. Morrill and J. Walter, 'Order and Disorder in the English Revolution', in A. Fletcher and J. Stevenson (eds.), *Order and Disorder in Early Modern England* (Cambridge, 1985).

CHAPTER VII
The Impact on Literature

Primary
Thomas Carew, *Poems*, ed. Rhodes Dunlap, Oxford, 1957.
Cavalier Poets, Selected Poems, ed. T. S. Clayton, Oxford, 1978.
John Cleveland, *Poems*, ed. B. Morris and Eleanor Withington, Oxford, 1967.
Abraham Cowley, *The Civil War*, ed. Allan Pritchard, Toronto, 1973.
——*The Poems*, ed. A. R. Waller, Cambridge, 1905.
George Daniel, *Poems*, ed. A. B. Grosart, 4 vols., 1878.
Samuel Daniel, *The Civil Wars Between the Houses of Lancaster and Yorke*, 1619, ed. Lawrence Michel, Yale University Press, 1958.
Sir William D'Avenant, *Gondibert* ed. D. F. Gladish, Oxford, 1971.
Fast Sermons to Parliament 1640–53, 34 vols., ed. Robin Jeffs in *The English Revolution 1640–53. I.*, 1970–1.
Robert Herrick, *The Poetical Works* ed. L. C. Martin, Oxford, 1963.
Thomas Hobbes, *Leviathan* ed. C. B. Macpherson, 1968.
Inigo Jones, *The Theatre of the Stuart Court*, 2 vols., ed. S. Orgel and R. Strong, Berkeley, 1973.
Richard Lovelace, *Poems*, ed. C. H. Wilkinson, Oxford, 1953.
Andrew Marvell, *Poems and Letters*, ed. H. M. Margoliouth, 1971.
Mercurius Aulicus, 4 vols., ed. Peter W. Thomas in *The English Revolution 1640–53. III*, 1971.

John Milton, *Complete Prose Works*, ed. D. M. Wolfe, New Haven, 1953–71.
——*Poems*, ed. J. Carey and A. Fowler, 1968.
The Thomason Tracts, British Library.
Henry Vaughan, *Complete Poems*, ed. Alan Rudrum, New Haven, 1976.
Edmund Waller, *Poems*, ed. G. Thorn-Drury, 1969.

Secondary
Raymond Anselment, *Loyalist Resolve, Patient Fortitude in the English Civil War*, 1988.
Douglas Brookes-Davies, *The Mercurian Monarch*, Manchester, 1983.
Douglas Bush, *English Literature in the Earlier 17th Century*, Oxford, 1962.
B. S. Capp, *Astrology and the Popular Press, English Almanacs, 1500–1800*, 1979.
Arthur E. Case, *A Bibliography of English Poetical Miscellanies 1521–1750*, Oxford, 1935.
Robert C. Elliott, *The Shape of Utopia*, Chicago, 1970.
Barbara Everett, 'The Shooting of the Bears: Poetry and politics in Andrew Marvell' in R. L. Brett, ed., *Andrew Marvell. Essays on the Tercentenary of his death*, Oxford, 1979.
Sir Charles Firth, *Cromwell's Army*, 1962 (1902).
G. K. Fortescue, *Catalogue of the Thomason Tracts*, 2 vols., 1908.
Joseph Frank, *The Beginnings of the English Newspaper, 1620–1660*, Cambridge, Mass., 1961.
——*Hobbled Pegasus. A Descriptive Bibliography of Minor English Poetry 1641–1660*, Albuquerque, 1968.
——*Cromwell's Press Agent: a critical biography of Marchmont Nedham 1620–78*, 1980.
Paul Fussell, *The Great War and Modern Memory*, Oxford, 1975.
Gerald Hammond, *Fleeting Things. English Poets and Poems 1616–1660*, Cambridge, Mass., 1990.
Hilton Kelliher, *Andrew Marvell. Poet and Politician, 1621–78*, 1978.
Carolyn Nelson and Matthew Seccombe, *British Newspapers and Periodicals 1641–1700, A Short-Title Catalogue*, Cambridge, Mass., 1987.
David Norbrook, *Poetry and Politics in the English Renaissance*, 1984.
W. R. Parker, *Milton A Biography*, 2 vols., Oxford, 1968.
Graham Parry, *The Seventeenth Century. The Intellectual and Cultural Context of English Literature 1603–1700*, 1989.
C. A. Patrides and J. Wittreich, eds., *The Apocalypse in English Renaissance Thought and Literature*, 1984.
T. J. Raylor, *The Achievement of Sir John Mennes and Dr James Smith*, unpublished Oxford D.Phil. thesis (1987).
Raman Selden, *English Verse Satire, 1590–1765*, 1978.
R. Shafer, *The English Ode to 1660*, Princeton, 1918.
Roy Sherwood, *The court of Oliver Cromwell*, 1977.
Nigel Smith, *Perfection Proclaimed. Language and Literature in English Radical Religion 1640–1660*, Oxford, 1989.
Peter W. Thomas, *Sir John Berkenhead 1617–79. A Royalist Career in Politics and Polemics*, Oxford, 1969.

——'Charles I of England. The Tragedy of Absolutism' in *The Courts of Europe*, ed. A. G. Dickens, 1977.

Peter Toon, *Puritans, the Millenium and the Future of Israel*, 1970.

James G. Turner, *The Politics of Landscape 1630–1660*, Oxford, 1978.

John Wordroper, *Love and Drollery*, 1969.

Blair Worden, 'The Politics of Marvell's Horatian Ode', *The Historical Journal*, vol. 27, 1984.

List of contributors

JOHN MORRILL is Fellow and Senior Tutor at Selwyn College, Cambridge and is the author of the seventeenth-century volume of the forthcoming *Oxford History of England*. His most recent book is *Oliver Cromwell and the English Revolution* (1990).

CHARLES CARLTON is professor of History at North Carolina State University. He is the author of several books including *Charles the First: the Personal Monarch* (1983) and *Archbishop William Laud* (1988) and is currently writing *Going to the Wars: the Experience of Civil War in the British Isles. 1638–1660*.

DAVID L. SMITH is Fellow of Selwyn College, Cambridge and in 1991 was Visiting Professor at the University of Chicago. He is the author of a study of Oliver Cromwell for sixth forms and is completing a book on Louis XIV and a study of Constitutional Royalism during the English Civil War.

GLENN BURGESS is Lecturer in History at the University of Canterbury, Christchurch, New Zealand. He is currently working on the interrelationships of English and Scottish political ideas in the sixteenth and seventeenth centuries. His forthcoming book is *The Politics of the Ancient Constitution: An Introduction to English Political Thought 1603–1642*.

IAN GENTLES is Associate Professor of History at Glendon College, York University, Toronto. His latest book is on the New Model Army, (1991).

JOHN WALTER is Lecturer in History and Director of the Local History Centre at the University of Essex. His most recent publication is *Famine, Disease and the Social Order in Early Modern Society* edited with Roger Schofield (1989) and he is completing a book on Popular Politics, Riot and Class in the English Revolution.

PETER W. THOMAS is Senior Lecturer in English at the University of Wales, College of Cardiff. He is the author of *Sir John Berkenhead: A Royalist Career in Politics and Polemics*. He is currently working on an edition of the poetry and prose of Cromwell's apologist, John Hall of Durham.

Illustration Acknowledgements

From *Historical Collections* published by John Rushworth (1682) 9: Fotomas 10: Mansell Collection 11: Fotomas 12: Mary Evans Picture Library 16, 18: Weidenfeld and Nicholson Ltd 22, 23, 25, 28: Ashmolean Museum, Oxford 31: History Today Archives 34, 37: Fotomas 38: Collins and Brown Archives 43: Fotomas 46: John R. Freeman 47: Fotomas 50: Weidenfeld and Nicholson Ltd 51: History Today Archives and Ashmolean Museum, Oxford 55: History Today Archives 56: Weidenfeld and Nicholson Ltd 58: History Today Archives 60: Collins and Brown Archives 64, 70: Fotomas 73: Collins and Brown Archives 79, 80: History Today Archives 83: Ian Gentles 85: Fotomas 89: by permission of the Provost and Fellows of Worcester College, Oxford 95: Weidenfeld and Nicholson Ltd 97: Collins and Brown Archives 98: Ian Gentles 103: Weidenfeld and Nicholson Ltd 106: Fotomas 111: courtesy of the Trustees of the British Library 114, 116: Collins and Brown Archives 118: Corpus Christi College Library, Oxford 126: History Today Archives 128: Weidenfeld and Nicholson Ltd 131: Mansell Collection 132: Weidenfeld and Nicholson Ltd 137.

Index